Notes Of Class Talks And Lectures-IV

by

Swami Vivekananda

Double9 BOOKS

Notes Of Class Talks And Lectures-IV

by Swami Vivekananda

ISBN: 978-93-59393-73-5

Published by

DOUBLE 9 BOOKS

2/13-B, Ansari Road
Daryaganj, New Delhi – 110002
info@double9books.com
www.double9books.com
Tel. 011-40042856

ABOUT THE AUTHOR

Swami Vivekananda was born Narendranath Datta in India on January 12, 1863. He died on July 4, 1902, and was the most important student of the Indian saint Ramakrishna. He was an important part of bringing Vedanta and Yoga to the West. He is also charged with making people more aware of other religions and making Hinduism a major world religion. Vivekananda had a lot of success at the Parliament. In the years that followed, he gave hundreds of lectures across the United States, England, and Europe to spread the main ideas of Hinduism. He also started the Vedanta Society of New York and the Vedanta Society of San Francisco, which is now the Vedanta Society of Northern California. Both of these groups became the basis for Vedanta Societies in the West. Vivekananda was one of the most important philosophers and social reformers in India at the time. He was also one of the most successful and powerful Vedanta missionaries in the West.People now think of him as one of the most important people in modern India and Hinduism. Mahatma Gandhi said that after reading Vivekananda's works, he loved his country a thousand times more.

CONTENTS

Notes Of Class Talks

WHEN WILL CHRIST COME AGAIN?

I never take much notice of these things. I have come to deal with principles. I have only to preach that God comes again and again, and that He came in India as Krishna, Râma, and Buddha, and that He will come again. It can almost be demonstrated that after each 500 years the world sinks, and a tremendous spiritual wave comes, and on the top of the wave is a Christ.

There is a great change now coming all over the world, and this is a cycle. Men are finding that they are losing hold of life; which way will they turn, down or up? Up, certainly. How can it be down? Plunge into the breach; fill up the breach with your body, your life. How should you allow the world to go down when you are living?

THE DIFFERENCE BETWEEN MAN AND CHRIST

There is much difference in manifested beings. As a manifested being you will never be Christ. Out of clay, manufacture a clay elephant, out of the same clay, manufacture a clay mouse. Soak them in water, they become one. As clay, they are eternally one; as fashioned things, they are eternally different. The Absolute is the material of both God and man. As Absolute, Omnipresent Being, we are all one; and as personal beings, God is the eternal master, and we are the eternal servants.

You have three things in you: (1) the body, (2) the mind, (3) the spirit. The spirit is intangible, the mind comes to birth and death, and so does the body. You are that spirit, but often you think you are the body. When a man says, "I am here", he thinks of the body. Then comes another moment when you are on the highest plane; you do not say, "I am here". But if a man abuses you or curses you and you do not resent it, you are the spirit. "When I think I am the mind, I am one spark of that eternal fire which Thou art; and when I feel that I am the spirit, Thou and I are one" — so says a devotee to the Lord. Is the mind in advance of the spirit?

God does not reason; why should you reason if you knew? It is a sign of weakness that we have to go on crawling like worms to get a few facts and build generalisations, and then the whole thing tumbles down again. The spirit is reflected in the mind and everything. It is the light of the spirit that makes the mind sensate. Everything is an expression of the spirit; the minds are so many mirrors. What you call love and fear, hatred, virtue, and vice are all reflections of the spirit; only when the reflector is base the reflection is bad.

ARE CHRIST AND BUDDHA IDENTICAL?

It is my particular fancy that the same Buddha became Christ. Buddha prophesied, "I will come again in five hundred years", and Christ came here in five hundred years. These are the two Lights of the whole human nature. Two men have been produced, Buddha and Christ; these are the two giants, huge gigantic personalities, two Gods. Between them they divide the whole world. Wherever there is the least knowledge in the world, people bow down either to Buddha or Christ. It would be very hard to produce more like them, but I hope there will be. Mohammed came five hundred years after, five hundred years after came Luther with his Protestant wave, and this is five hundred years after that again. It is a great thing in a few thousand years to produce two such men as Jesus and Buddha. Are not two such enough? Christ and Buddha were Gods, the others were prophets. Study the life of these two and see the manifestation of power in them — calm and non-resisting, poor beggars owning nothing, without a cent in their pockets, despised all their lives, called heretic and fool — and think of the immense spiritual power they have wielded over humanity.

SALVATION FROM SIN

We are to be saved from sin by being saved from ignorance. Ignorance is the cause of which sin is the result.

COMING BACK TO THE DIVINE MOTHER

When a nurse takes a baby out into the garden and plays with the baby, the Mother may send a word to the baby to come indoors. The baby is absorbed in play, and says, "I won't come; I don't want to eat." After a while the baby becomes tired with his play and says, "I will go to Mother." The nurse says, "Here is a new doll", but the baby says, "I don't care for dolls any more. I will go to Mother", and he weeps until he goes. We are all babies. The Mother is God. We are absorbed in seeking for money, wealth, and all these things; but the time will come when we will awaken; and then this nature will try to give us more dolls, and we will say, "No, I have had enough; I will go to God."

NO INDIVIDUALITY APART FROM GOD

If we are inseparable from God, and always one, have we no individuality? Oh yes; that is God. Our individuality is God. This is not real individuality which you have now. You are coming towards that true one. Individuality means what cannot be divided. How can you call this state — we are now — individuality? One hour you are thinking one way, and the next hour another way, and two hours after another way. Individuality is that which changes not. It would be tremendously dangerous for the present state to remain in eternity, then the thief would always remain a thief, and the blackguard, a blackguard. If a baby died, it would have to remain a baby. The real individuality is that which never changes, and will never change; and that is God within us.

Man The Maker Of His Destiny

There was a very powerful dynasty in Southern India. They made it a rule to take the horoscope of all the prominent men living from time to time, calculated from the time of their birth. In this way they got a record of leading facts predicted, and compared them afterwards with events as they happened. This was done for a thousand years, until they found certain agreements; these were generalised and recorded and made into a huge book. The dynasty died out, but the family of astrologers lived and had the book in their possession. It seems possible that this is how astrology came into existence. Excessive attention to the minutiae of astrology is one of the superstitions which has hurt the Hindus very much.

I think the Greeks first took astrology to India and took from the Hindus the science of astronomy and carried it back with them from Europe. Because in India you will find old altars made according to a certain geometrical plan, and certain things had to be done when the stars were in certain positions, therefore I think the Greeks gave the Hindus astrology, and the Hindus gave them astronomy.

I have seen some astrologers who predicted wonderful things; but I have no reason to believe they predicted them only from the stars, or anything of the sort. In many cases it is simply mind-reading. Sometimes wonderful predictions are made, but in many cases it is arrant trash.

In London, a young man used to come to me and ask me, "What will become of me next year?" I asked him why he asked me so. "I have lost all my money and have become very, very poor." Money is the only God of many beings. Weak men, when they lose everything and feel themselves weak, try all sorts of uncanny methods of making money, and come to astrology and all these things. "It is the coward and the fool who says, 'This is fate'" — so says the Sanskrit proverb. But it is the strong man who stands up and says, "I will make my fate." It is people who are getting old who talk of fate. Young men generally do not come to astrology. We *may* be under planetary influence, but it should not matter much to us. Buddha says, "Those that get a living by calculation of the stars by such art and other lying tricks are to be avoided"; and he ought to know, because he was the greatest Hindu ever born. Let stars come, what harm is there? If a star disturbs my life, it would not be worth a cent. You will find that astrology and all these mystical things are generally signs of a weak mind; therefore as soon as they are becoming prominent in our minds, we should see a physician, take good food and rest.

If you can get an explanation of a phenomenon from within its nature, it is nonsense to look for an explanation from outside. If the world explains itself, it is nonsense to go outside for an explanation. Have you found any phenomena in the life of a man that you have ever seen which cannot be explained by the power of the man himself? So what is the use of going to the stars or anything else in the world? My own Karma is sufficient explanation of my present state. So in the case of Jesus himself. We know that his father was only a carpenter. We need not go to anybody else to find an explanation of his power. He was the outcome of his own past, all of which was a preparation for that Jesus. Buddha goes back and back to animal bodies and tells us how he ultimately became Buddha. So what is the use of going to stars for explanation? They may have a little influence; but it is our duty to ignore them rather than hearken to them and make ourselves nervous. This I lay down as the first essential in all I teach: anything that brings spiritual, mental, or physical weakness, touch it not with the toes of your feet. Religion is the manifestation of the natural strength that is in man. A spring of infinite power is coiled up and is inside this little body, and that spring is spreading itself. And as it goes on spreading, body after body is found insufficient; it throws them off and takes higher bodies. This is the history of man, of religion, civilisation, or progress. That giant Prometheus, who is bound, is getting himself unbound. It is always a manifestation of strength, and all these ideas such as astrology, although there may be a grain of truth in them, should be avoided.

There is an old story of an astrologer who came to a king and said, "You are going to die in six months." The king was frightened out of his wits and was almost about to die then and there from fear. But his minister was a clever man, and this man told the king that these astrologers were fools. The king would not believe him. So the minister saw no other way to make the king see that they were fools but to invite the astrologer to the palace again. There he asked him if his calculations were correct. The astrologer said that there could not be a mistake, but to satisfy him he went through the whole of the calculations again and then said that they were perfectly correct. The king's face became livid. The minister said to the astrologer, "And when do you think that you will die?" "In twelve years", was the reply. The minister quickly drew his sword and separated the astrologer's head from the body and said to the king, "Do you see this liar? He is dead this moment."

If you want your nation to live, keep away from all these things. The only test of good things is that they make us strong. Good is life, evil is death. These superstitious ideas are springing like mushrooms in your country, and women wanting in logical analysis of things are ready to believe them. It is because women are striving for liberation, and women have not yet established themselves intellectually. One gets by heart a few lines of poetry from the top of a novel and says she knows the whole of Browning. Another attends a course of three lectures and then thinks she knows everything in the world. The difficulty is that they are unable to throw off the natural superstition of women. They have a lot of money and some intellectual learning, but when they have passed through this transition stage and get on firm ground, they will be all right. But they are played upon by charlatans. Do not be sorry; I do not mean to hurt anyone, but I have to tell the truth. Do you not see how open you are to these things? Do you not see how sincere these women are, how that divinity latent in all never dies? It is only to know how to appeal to the Divine.

The more I live, the more I become convinced every day that every human being is divine. In no man or woman, however vile, does that divinity die. Only he or she does not know how to reach it and is waiting for the Truth. And wicked people are trying to deceive him or her with all sorts of fooleries. If one man cheats another for money, you say he is a fool and a blackguard. How much greater is the iniquity of one who wants to fool others spiritually! This is too bad. It is the one test, that truth must make you strong and put you above superstition. The duty of the philosopher is to raise you above superstition. Even this world, this body and mind are superstitions; what infinite souls you are! And to be tricked by twinkling stars! It is a shameful condition. You are divinities; the twinkling stars owe their existence to you.

I was once travelling in the Himalayas, and the long road stretched before us. We poor monks cannot get any one to carry us, so we had to make all the way on foot. There was an old man with us. The way goes up and down for hundreds of miles, and when that old monk saw what was before him, he said, "Oh sir, how to cross it; I cannot walk any more; my chest will break." I said to him, "Look down at your feet." He did so, and I said, "The road that is under your feet is the road that you have passed over and is the same road that you see before you; it will soon be under your feet." The highest things are under your feet, because you are Divine Stars; all these things are under your feet. You can swallow the stars by the handful if you want; such is your real nature. Be strong, get beyond all superstitions, and be free.

God: Personal And Impersonal

My idea is that what you call a Personal God is the same as the Impersonal Being, a Personal and Impersonal God at the same time. We are personalised impersonal beings. If you use the word in the absolute sense, we are impersonal; but if you use it in a relative meaning, we are personal. Each one of you is a universal being, each one is omnipresent. It may seem staggering at first, but I am as sure of this as that I stand before you. How can the spirit help being omnipresent? It has neither length, nor breadth, nor thickness, nor any material attribute whatsoever; and if we are all spirits we cannot be limited by space. Space only limits space, matter matter. If we were limited to this body we would be a material something. Body and soul and everything would be material, and such words as "living in the body", "embodying the soul" would be only words used for convenience; beyond that they would have no meaning. Many of you remember the definition I gave of the soul; that each soul is a circle whose centre is in one point and circumference nowhere. The centre is where the body is, and the activity is manifested there. You are omnipresent; only you have the consciousness of being concentrated in one point. That point has taken up particles of matter, and formed them into a machine to express itself. That through which it expresses itself is called the body. So you are everywhere; when one body or machine fails, you, the centre, move on and take up other particles of matter, finer or grosser, and work through that. This is man. And what is God? God is a circle with its circumference nowhere and centre everywhere. Every point in that circle is living, conscious, active, and equally working; with us limited souls, only one point is conscious, and that point moves forward and backward. As the body has a very infinitesimal existence in comparison with that of the universe, so the whole universe, in comparison with God, is nothing. When we talk of God speaking, we say He speaks through His universe; and when we speak of Him beyond all limitations of time and space, we say He is an Impersonal Being. Yet He is the same Being.

To give an illustration: We stand here and see the sun. Suppose you want to go towards the sun. After you get a few thousand miles nearer, you will see another sun, much bigger. Supposing you proceed much closer, you will see a much bigger sun. At last you will see the real sun, millions and millions of miles big. Suppose you divide this journey into so many stages, and take photographs from each stage, and after you have taken the real sun, come back and compare them; they will all appear to be different, because the first view was a little red ball, and the real sun was millions of miles bigger; yet it was the same sun. It is the same with God: the Infinite Being we see from different standpoints, from different planes of mind. The lowest man sees Him as an ancestor; as his vision gets higher, as the Governor of the planet; still higher as the Governor of the universe, and the highest man sees Him as himself. It was the same God, and the different realisations were only degrees and differences of vision.

The Divine Incarnation Or Avatara

Jesus Christ was God — the Personal God become man. He has manifested Himself many times in different forms and these alone are what you can worship. God in His absolute nature is not to be worshipped. Worshipping such God would be nonsense. We have to worship Jesus Christ, the human manifestation, as God. You cannot worship anything higher than the manifestation of God. The sooner you give up the worship of God separate from Christ, the better for you. Think of the Jehovah you manufacture and of the beautiful Christ. Any time you attempt to make a God beyond Christ, you murder the whole thing. God alone can worship God. It is not given to man, and any attempt to worship Him beyond His ordinary manifestations will be dangerous to mankind. Keep close to Christ if you want salvation; He is higher than any God you can imagine. If you think that Christ was a man, do not worship Him; but as soon as you can realise that He is God, worship Him. Those who say He was a man and then worship Him commit blasphemy; there is no half-way house for you; you must take the whole strength of it. "He that hath seen the Son hath seen the Father", and without seeing the Son, you *cannot* see the Father. It would be only tall talk and frothy philosophy and dreams and speculations. But if you want to have a hold on spiritual life, cling close to God as manifest in Christ.

Philosophically speaking, there was no such human being living as Christ or Buddha; we saw God through them. In the Koran, Mohammed again and again repeats that Christ was never crucified, it was a semblance; no one could crucify Christ.

The lowest state of philosophical religion is dualism; the highest form is the Triune state. Nature and the human soul are interpenetrated by God, and this we see as the Trinity of God, nature, and soul. At the same time you catch a glimpse that all these three are products of the One. Just as this body is the covering of the soul, so this is, as it were, the body of God. As I am the soul of nature, so is God the soul of my soul. You are the centre through which you see all nature in which you are. This nature, soul, and God make one individual being, the universe. Therefore they are a unity; yet at the same time they are separate. Then there is another sort of Trinity which is much like the Christian Trinity. God is absolute. We cannot see God in His absolute nature, we can only speak of that as "not this, not this". Yet we can get certain qualities as the nearest approach to God. First is existence, second is knowledge, third is bliss — very much corresponding to your Father, Son, and Holy Ghost. Father is the existence out of which everything comes; Son is that knowledge. It is in Christ that God will be manifest. God was everywhere, in all beings, before Christ; but in Christ we became conscious of Him. This is God. The third is bliss, the Holy Spirit. As soon as you get this knowledge, you get bliss. As soon as you begin to have Christ within you, you have bliss; and that unifies the three.

Pranayama

First of all we will try to understand a little of the meaning of Prânâyama. Prâna stands in metaphysics for the sum total of the energy that is in the universe. This universe, according to the theory of the philosophers, proceeds in the form of waves; it rises, and again it subsides, melts away, as it were; then again it proceeds out in all this variety; then again it slowly returns. So it goes on like a pulsation. The whole of this universe is composed of matter and force; and according to Sanskrit philosophers, everything that we call matter, solid and liquid, is the outcome of one primal matter which they call Âkâsha or ether; and the primordial force, of which all the forces that we see in nature are manifestations, they call Prana. It is this Prana acting upon Akasha, which creates this universe, and after the end of a period, called a cycle, there is a period of rest. One period of activity is followed by a period of rest; this is the nature of everything. When this period of rest comes, all these forms that we see in the earth, the sun, the moon, and the stars, all these manifestations melt down until they become ether again. They become dissipated as ether. All these forces, either in the body or in the mind, as gravitation, attraction, motion, thought, become dissipated, and go off into the primal Prana. We can understand from this the importance of this Pranayama. Just as this ether encompasses us everywhere and we are interpenetrated by it, so everything we see is composed of this ether, and we are floating in the ether like pieces of ice floating in a lake. They are formed of the water of the lake and float in it at the same time. So everything that exists is composed of this Akasha and is floating in this ocean. In the same way we are surrounded by this vast ocean of Prana — force and energy. It is this Prana by which we breathe and by which the circulation of the blood goes on; it is the energy in the nerves and in the muscles, and the thought in the brain. All forces are different manifestations of this same Prana, as all matter is a different manifestation of the same Akasha. We always find the causes of the gross in the subtle. The chemist takes a solid lump of ore and analyses it; he wants to find the subtler things out of which that gross is composed. So with our thought and our knowledge; the explanation of the grosser is in the finer. The effect is the gross and the cause the subtle. This gross universe of ours, which we see, feel, and touch, has its cause and explanation behind in the thought. The cause and explanation of that is also further behind. So in this human body of ours, we first find the gross movements, the movements of the hands and lips; but where are the causes of these? The finer nerves, the movements of which we cannot perceive at all, so fine that we cannot see or touch or trace them in any way with our senses, and yet we know they are the cause of these grosser movements. These nerve movements, again, are caused by still finer movements, which we call thought; and that is caused by something finer still behind, which is the soul of man, the Self, the Âtman. In order to understand ourselves we have first to make our perception fine. No microscope or instrument that was ever invented will make it possible for us to see the fine movements that are going on inside; we can never see them by any such means. So the Yogi has a science that manufactures an instrument for the study of his own mind, and that instrument is in the mind. The mind attains to powers of finer perception which no instrument will ever be able to attain.

To attain to this power of superfine perception we have to begin from the gross. And as the power becomes finer and finer, we go deeper and deeper inside our own nature; and all the gross movements will first be tangible to us, and then the finer movements of the thought; we will be able to trace the thought before its beginning, trace it where it goes and where it ends. For instance, in the ordinary mind a thought arises. The mind does not know how it began or whence it comes. The mind is like the ocean in which a wave rises, but although the man sees the wave, he does not know how the wave came there, whence its birth, or whither it melts down again; he cannot trace it any further. But when the perception becomes finer, we can trace this wave long, long before it comes to the surface; and we will be able to trace it for a long distance after it has disappeared, and then we can understand psychology as it truly is. Nowadays men think this or that and write many volumes, which are entirely misleading, because they have not the power to analyse their own minds and are talking of things they have never *known*, but only theorised about. All science must be based on facts, and these facts must be observed and generalised. Until you have some facts to generalise upon, what are you going to do? So all these attempts at generalising are based upon knowing the things we generalise. A man proposes a theory, and adds theory to theory, until the whole book is patchwork of theories, not one of them with the least meaning. The science of Râja-Yoga says, first you must gather facts about your own mind, and that can be done by analysing your mind, developing its finer powers of perception and seeing for yourselves what is happening inside; and when you have got these facts, then generalise; and then alone you will have the real science of psychology.

As I have said, to come to any finer perception we must take the help of the grosser end of it. The current of action which is manifested on the outside is the grosser. If we can get hold of this and go on further and further, it becomes finer and finer, and at last the finest. So this body and everything we have in this body are not different existences, but, as it were, various links in the same chain proceeding from fine to gross. You are a complete whole; this body is the outside manifestation, the crust, of the inside; the external is grosser and the inside finer; and so finer and finer until you come to the Self. And at last, when we come to the Self, we come to know that it was only the Self that was manifesting all this; that it was the Self which became the mind and became the body; that nothing else exists but the Self, and all these others are manifestations of that Self in various degrees, becoming grosser and grosser. So we will find by analogy that in this whole universe there is the gross manifestation, and behind that is the finer movement, which we can call the will of God. Behind that even, we will find that Universal Self. And then we will come to know that the Universal Self becomes God and becomes this universe; and that it is not that this universe is one and God another and the Supreme Self another, but that they are different states of the manifestation of the same Unity behind.

All this comes of our Pranayama. These finer movements that are going on inside the body are connected with the breathing; and if we can get hold of this breathing and manipulate it and control it, we will slowly get to finer and finer motions, and thus enter, as it were, by getting hold of that breathing, into the realms of the mind.

The first breathing that I taught you in our last lesson was simply an exercise for the time being. Some of these breathing exercises, again, are very difficult, and I will try to avoid all the difficult ones, because the more difficult ones require a great deal of dieting and other restrictions which it is impossible for most of you to keep to. So we will take the slower paths and the simpler ones. This breathing consists of three parts. The first is breathing in, which is called in Sanskrit Puraka, filling; and the second part is called Kumbhaka, retaining, filling the lungs and stopping the air from coming out; the third is called Rechaka, breathing out. The first exercise which I will give you today is simply breathing in and stopping the breath and throwing it out slowly. Then there is one step more in the breathing which I will not give you today, because you cannot remember them all; it would be too intricate. These three parts of breathing make one Pranayama. This breathing should be regulated, because if it is not, there is danger in the way to yourselves. So it is regulated by numbers, and I will give you first the lowest numbers. Breathe in four seconds, then hold the breath for eight seconds, then again throw it out slowly in four seconds. (This process is more difficult when the ratio is two, eight, and four: for further remarks see later.) Then begin again, and do this four times in the morning and four times in the evening. There is one thing more. Instead of counting by one, two, three, and all such meaningless things, it is better to repeat any word that is holy to you. In our country we have symbolical words, "Om" for instance, which means God. If that be pronounced instead of one, two, three, four, it will serve your purpose very well. One thing more. This breathing should begin through the left nostril and should turn out through the right nostril, and the next time is should be drawn in through the right and thrown out through the left. Then reverse again, and so on. In the first place you should be able to drive your breathing through either nostril at will, just by the power of the will. After a time you will find it easy; but now I am afraid you have not that power. So we must stop the one nostril while breathing through the other with the finger and during the retention, of course, both nostrils.

The first two lessons should not be forgotten. The first thing is to hold yourselves straight; second to think of the body as sound and perfect, as healthy and strong. Then throw a current of love all around, think of the whole universe being happy. Then if you believe in God, pray. Then breathe.

In many of you certain physical changes will come, twitchings all over the body, nervousness; some of you will feel like weeping, sometimes a violent motion will come. Do not be afraid; these things have to come as you go on practicing. The whole body will have to be rearranged as it were. New channels for thought will be made in the brain, nerves which have not acted in your whole life will begin to work, and a whole new series of changes will come in the body itself.

Women Of The East

(As many women as could crowd into Hall 7 yesterday afternoon flocked thither to hear something as to the lives of their sisters of the Orient. Mrs. Potter Palmer and Mrs. Charles Henrotin sat upon the platform, surrounded by turbanned representatives of the women of the East.

It may interest the readers to know that the published addresses of Swami Vivekananda at the Parliament of Religions in Chicago are not exhaustive and many addresses, specially those delivered at the Scientific Section of the Parliament were not all reported. The Scientific Sessions were conducted simultaneously with the open session at the Hall of Columbus. Swami Vivekananda spoke on the following subjects at the Scientific Section:

1. Orthodox Hinduism and the Vedanta Philosophy.
   — *Friday, September 22, 1893, at 10-30 a.m.*
2. The Modern Religions of India.
   — *Friday, September 22, 1893 afternoon session.*
3. On the subject of the foregoing addresses.
   — *Saturday, September 23, 1893.*
4. The Essence of the Hindu Religion.
   — *Monday, September 25, 1893.*

The Chicago Daily Inter-Ocean of September 23, 1893 published the following note on the first lecture.

"In the Scientific Section yesterday morning Swami Vivekananda spoke on 'Orthodox Hinduism'. Hall III was crowded to overflowing and hundreds of questions were asked by auditors and answered by the great Sannyasin with wonderful skill and lucidity. At the close of the session he was thronged with eager questions who begged him to give a semi-public lecture somewhere on the subject of his religion. He said that he already had the project under consideration.")

(Report of a lecture in the Chicago Daily Inter-Ocean, September 23, 1893)

Swami Vivekananda, at a special meeting, discussed the present and future of the women of the East. He said, "The best thermometer to the progress of a nation is its treatment of its women. In ancient Greece there was absolutely no difference in the state of man and woman. The idea of perfect equality existed. No Hindu can be a priest until he is married, the idea being that a single man is only half a man, and imperfect. The idea of perfect womanhood is perfect independence. The central idea of the life of a modern Hindu lady is her chastity. The wife is the centre of a circle, the fixity of which depends upon her chastity. It was the extreme of this idea which caused Hindu widows to be burnt. The Hindu women are very spiritual and very religious, perhaps more so than any other women in the world. If we can preserve these beautiful characteristics and at the same time develop the intellects of our women, the Hindu woman of the future will be the ideal woman of the world."

Congress Of Religious Unity

(Report of a lecture in the Chicago Sunday Herald, September 24, 1893)

Swami Vivekananda said, "All the words spoken at this parliament come to the common conclusion that the brotherhood of man is the much-to-be-desired end. Much has been said for this brotherhood as being a natural condition, since we are all children of one God. Now, there are sects that do not admit of the existence of God — that is, a Personal God. Unless we wish to leave those sects out in the cold — and in that case our brotherhood will not be universal — we must have our platform broad enough to embrace all mankind. It has been said here that we should do good to our fellow men, because every bad or mean deed reacts on the doer. This appears to me to savour of the shopkeeper — ourselves first, our brothers afterwards. I think we should love our brother whether we believe in the universal fatherhood of God or not, because every religion and every creed recognises man as divine, and you should do him no harm that you might not injure that which is divine in him."

The Love Of God-I

(Report of a lecture in the Chicago Herald, September 25, 1893)

An audience that filled the auditorium of the Third Unitarian Church at Laflin and Monroe streets heard Swami Vivekananda preach yesterday morning. The subject of his sermon was the love of God, and his treatment of the theme was eloquent and unique. He said that God was worshipped in all parts of the world, but by different names and in different ways. It is natural for men, he said, to worship the grand and the beautiful, and that religion was a portion of their nature. The need of God was felt by all, and His love prompted them to deeds of charity, mercy, and justice. All men loved God because He was love itself. The speaker had heard since coming to Chicago a great deal about the brotherhood of man. He believed that a still stronger tie connected them, in that all are the offsprings of the love of God. The brotherhood of man was the logical sequence of God as the Father of all. The speaker said he had travelled in the forests of India and slept in caves, and from his observation of nature he had drawn the belief that there was something above the natural law that kept men from wrong, and that, he concluded, was the love of God. If God had spoken to Christ, Mohammed, and the Rishis of the Vedas, why did He not speak also to him, one of his children?

"Indeed, he does speak to me", the Swami continued, "and to all His children. We see Him all around us and are impressed continually by the boundlessness of His love, and from that love we draw the inspiration for our well-being and well-doing."

The Love Of God-II

(A lecture delivered in the Unitarian Church of Detroit
on February 20, 1894
and reported in the Detroit Free Press)

Vivekananda delivered a lecture on "The Love of God" at the Unitarian Church last night before the largest audience that he has yet had. The trend of the lecturer's remarks was to show that we do not accept God because we really want Him, but because we have need of Him for selfish purposes. Love, said the speaker, is something absolutely unselfish, that which has no thought beyond the glorification and adoration of the object upon which our affections are bestowed. It is a quality which bows down and worships and asks nothing in return. Merely to love is the sole request that true love has to ask.

It is said of a Hindu saint that when she was married, she said to her husband, the king, that she was already married. "To whom?" asked the king. "To God", was the reply. She went among the poor and the needy and taught the doctrine of extreme love for God. One of her prayers is significant, showing the manner in which her heart was moved: "I ask not for wealth; I ask not for position; I ask not for salvation; place me in a hundred hells if it be Thy wish, but let me continue to regard Thee as my love." The early language abounds in beautiful prayers of this woman. When her end came, she entered into Samâdhi on the banks of a river. She composed a beautiful song, in which she stated that she was going to meet her Beloved.

Men are capable of philosophical analysis of religion. A woman is devotional by nature and loves God from the heart and soul and not from the mind. The songs of Solomon are one of the most beautiful parts of the Bible. The language in them is much of that affectionate kind which is found in the prayers of the Hindu woman saint. And yet I have heard that Christians are going to have these incomparable songs removed. I have heard an explanation of the songs in which it is said that Solomon loved a young girl and desired her to return his royal affection. The girl, however, loved a young man and did not want to have anything to do with Solomon. This explanation is excellent to some people, because they cannot understand such wondrous love for God as is embodied in the songs. Love for God in India is different from love for God elsewhere, because when you get into a country where the thermometer reads 40 degrees below zero, the temperament of the people changes. The aspirations of the people in the climate where the books of the Bible are said to have been written were different from the aspirations of the cold-blooded Western nations, who are more apt to worship the almighty dollar with the warmth expressed in the songs than to worship God. Love for God seems to be based upon a basis of "what can I get out of it?" In their prayers they ask for all kinds of selfish things.

Christians are always wanting God to give them something. They appear as beggars before the throne of the Almighty. A story is told of a beggar who applied to an emperor for alms. While he was waiting, it was time for the emperor to offer up prayers. The emperor prayed, "O God, give me more wealth; give me more power; give me a greater empire." The beggar started to leave. The emperor turned and asked him, "Why are you going?" "I do not beg of beggars", was the reply.

Some people find it really difficult to understand the frenzy of religious fervour which moved the heart of Mohammed. He would grovel in the dust and writhe in agony. Holy men who have experienced these extreme emotions have been called epileptic. The absence of the thought of self is the essential characteristic of the love for God. Religion nowadays has become a mere hobby and fashion. People go to church like a flock of sheep. They do not embrace God because they need Him. Most persons are unconscious atheists who self-complacently think that they are devout believers.

India

(Report of a lecture delivered at Detroit on Thursday, February 15, 1894, with the editorial comments of the Detroit Free Press)

An audience that filled the Unitarian Church heard the renowned monk, Swami Vivekananda, deliver a lecture last night on the manners and customs of his country. His eloquent and graceful manner pleased his listeners, who followed him from beginning to end with the closest attention, showing approval from time to time by outbursts of applause. While his lecture was more popular in character than the celebrated Address before the religious congress in Chicago, it was highly entertaining, especially where the speaker diverted from the instructive portions and was led to an eloquent narration of certain spiritual conditions of his own people. It is upon matters religious and philosophic (and necessarily spiritual) that the Eastern brother is most impressive, and, while outlining the duties that follow the conscientious consideration of the great moral law of nature, his softly modulated tones, a peculiarity of his people, and his thrilling manner are almost prophetic. He speaks with marked deliberation, except when placing before his listeners some moral truth, and then his eloquence is of the highest kind.

It seemed somewhat singular that the Eastern monk, who is so outspoken in his disapproval of missionary labour on the part of the Christian church in India (where, he affirms, the morality is the highest in the world), should have been introduced by Bishop Ninde who in June will depart for China in the interest of foreign Christian missions. The Bishop expects to remain away until December; but if he should stay longer he will go to India. The Bishop referred to the wonders of India and the intelligence of the educated classes there, introducing Vivekananda in a happy manner. When that dusky gentleman arose, dressed in his turban and bright gown, with handsome face and bright, intelligent eyes, he presented an impressive figure. He returned thanks to the Bishop for his words and proceeded to explain race divisions in his own country, the manners of the people, and the different languages. Principally there are four northern tongues and four southern, but there is one common religion. Four-fifths of the population of 300 million people are Hindus and the Hindu is a peculiar person. He does everything in a religious manner. He eats religiously; he sleeps religiously; he rises in the morning religiously; he does good things religiously; and he also does bad things religiously. At this point the lecturer struck the great moral keynote of his discourse, stating that with his people it was the belief that all non-self is good and all self is bad. This point was emphasised throughout the evening and might be termed the text of the address. To build a home is selfish, argues the Hindu; so he builds it for the worship of God and for the entertainment of guests. To cook food is selfish, so he cooks for the poor; he will serve himself last if any hungry stranger applies, and this feeling extends throughout the length and breadth of the land. Any man can ask for food and shelter, and any house will be opened to him.

The caste system has nothing to do with religion. A man's occupation is hereditary: a carpenter is born a carpenter; a goldsmith, a goldsmith; a workman, a workman; and a priest, a priest. But this is a comparatively modern social evil, since it has existed only about 1,000 years. This period of time does not seem so great in India as in this and other countries. Two gifts are especially appreciated — the gift of learning and the gift of life. But the gift of learning takes precedence. One may save a man's life, and that is excellent; one may impart to another knowledge, and that is better. To instruct for money is an evil, and to do this would bring opprobrium on the head of the man who barters learning for gold, as though it were an article of trade. The government makes gifts from time to time to the instructors, and the moral effect is better than it would be if the conditions were the same as exist in certain alleged civilised countries. The speaker had asked through the length and breadth of the land what was the definition of civilisation, and he had asked the question in many countries. Sometimes the reply had been given: What we are, that is civilisation. He begged to differ in the definition of the word. A nation may control the elements, develop utilitarian problems of life seemingly to the limit, and yet not realise that in the individual the highest type of civilisation is found in him who has learnt to conquer self. This condition is found in India more than in any country on earth, for there the material conditions are subservient to the spiritual, and the individual looks for the soul manifestations in everything that has life, studying nature to this end. Hence that gentle disposition to endure with indomitable patience the flings of what appears unkind fortune, the while there is a full consciousness of a spiritual strength and knowledge greater than those possessed by any other people; hence the existence of a country and a people from which flows an unending stream that attracts the attention of thinkers far and near to approach and throw from their shoulders an oppressive earthly burden. The early king, who in 260 B.C. commanded that there should be no more bloodshed, no more wars, and who sent forth instead of soldiers an army of instructors, acted wisely, although in material things the land has suffered. But though in bondage to brutal nations who conquer by force, the Indian's spirituality endures for ever, and nothing can take it away from him. There is something Christlike in the humility of the people to endure the stings and arrows of outraged fortune, the while the soul is advancing towards the brighter goal. Such a country has no need of Christian missionaries to "preach ideas", for theirs is a religion that makes men gentle, sweet, considerate, and affectionate towards all God's creatures, whether man or beast. Morally, said the speaker, India is head and shoulders above the United States or any other country on the globe. Missionaries would do well to come there and drink of the pure waters, and see what a beautiful influence upon a great community have the lives of the multitude of holy men.

Then marriage condition was described; and the privileges extended to women in ancient times when the system of co-education flourished. In the records of the saints in India there is the unique figure of the prophetess. In the Christian creed they are all prophets, while in India the holy women occupy a conspicuous place in the holy books. The householder has five objects for worship. One of them is learning and teaching. Another is worship of dumb creatures. It is hard for Americans to understand the last worship, and it is difficult for Europeans to appreciate the sentiment. Other nations kill animals by wholesale and kill one another; they exist in a sea of blood. A European said that the reason why in India animals were not killed was because it was supposed that they contained the spirits of ancestors. This reason was worthy of a savage nation who are not many steps from the brute. The fact was that the statement was made by a set of atheists in India who thus carped at the Vedic idea of non-killing and transmigration of souls. It was never a religious doctrine, it was an idea of a materialistic creed. The worship of dumb animals was pictured in a vivid manner. The hospitable spirit — the Indian golden rule, was illustrated by a story. A Brâhmin, his wife, his son, and his son's wife had not tasted food for some time on account of a famine. The head of the house went out and after a search found a small quantity of barley. He brought this home and divided it into four portions, and the small family was about to eat, when a knock was heard at the door. It was a guest. The different portions were set before him, and he departed with his hunger satisfied, while the quartette who had entertained him perished. This story is told in India to illustrate what is expected in the sacred name of hospitality.

The speaker concluded in an eloquent manner. Throughout, his speech was simple; but whenever he indulged in imagery, it was delightfully poetic, showing that the Eastern brother has been a close and attentive observer of the beauties of nature. His excessive spirituality is a quality which makes itself felt with his auditors, for it manifests itself in the love for animate and inanimate things and in the keen insight into the mysterious workings of the divine law of harmony and kindly intentions.

Hindus And Christians

(A lecture delivered at Detroit on February 21, 1894, and reported in the Detroit Free Press)

Of the different philosophies, the tendency of the Hindu is not to destroy, but to harmonise everything. If any new idea comes into India, we do not antagonise it, but simply try to take it in, to harmonise it, because this method was taught first by our prophet, God incarnate on earth, Shri Krishna. This Incarnation of God preached himself first: "I am the God Incarnate, I am the inspirer of all books, I am the inspirer of all religions." Thus we do not reject any.

There is one thing which is very dissimilar between us and Christians, something which we never taught. That is the idea of salvation through Jesus' blood, or cleansing by any man's blood. We had our sacrifice as the Jews had. Our sacrifices mean simply this: Here is some food I am going to eat, and until some portion is offered to God, it is bad; so I offer the food. This is the pure and simple idea. But with the Jew the idea is that his sin be upon the lamb, and let the lamb be sacrificed and him go scot-free. We never developed this beautiful idea in India, and I am glad we did not. I, for one, would not come to be saved by such a doctrine. If anybody would come and say, "Be saved by my blood", I would say to him, "My brother, go away; I will go to hell; I am not a coward to take innocent blood to go to heaven; I am ready for hell." So that doctrine never cropped up amongst us, and our prophet says that whenever evil and immortality prevail on earth, He will come down and support His children; and this He is doing from time to time and from place to place. And whenever on earth you see an extraordinary holy man trying to uplift humanity, know that He is in him.

So you see that is the reason why we never fight any religion. We do not say that ours is the only way to salvation. Perfection can be had by everybody, and what is the proof? Because we see the holiest of men in all countries, good men and women everywhere, whether born in our faith or not. Therefore it cannot be held that ours is the only way to salvation. "Like so many rivers flowing from different mountains, all coming and mingling their waters in the sea, all the different religions, taking their births from different standpoints of fact, come unto Thee." This is a part of the child's everyday prayer in India. With such everyday prayers, of course, such ideas as fighting because of differences of religion are simply impossible. So much for the philosophers of India. We have great regard for all these men, especially this prophet, Shri Krishna, on account of his wonderful catholicity in harmonising all the preceding revelations.

Then the man who is bowing down before the idol. It is not in the same sense as you have heard of the Babylonian and the Roman idolatry. It is peculiar to the Hindus. The man is before the idol, and he shuts his eyes and tries to think, "I am He; I have neither life nor death; I have neither father nor mother; I am not bound by time or space; I am Existence infinite, Bliss infinite, and Knowledge infinite; I am He, I am He. I am not bound by books, or holy places, or pilgrimages, or anything whatsoever; I am the Existence Absolute, Bliss Absolute; I am He, I am He." This he repeats and then says, "O Lord, I cannot conceive Thee in myself; I am a poor man." Religion does not depend upon knowledge. It is the soul itself, it is God, not to be attained by simple book-knowledge or powers of speech. You may take the most learned man you have and ask him to think of spirit as spirit; he cannot. You may imagine spirit, he may imagine spirit. It is impossible to think of spirit without training. So no matter how much theology you may learn — you may be a great philosopher and greater theologian — but the Hindu boy would say, "Well, that has nothing to do with religion." Can you think of spirit as spirit? Then alone all doubt ceases, and all crookedness of the heart is made straight. Then only all fears vanish, and all doubtings are for ever silent when man's soul and God come face to face.

A man may be wonderfully learned in the Western sense, yet he may not know the A B C of religion. I would tell him that. I would ask him, "Can you think of spirit as such? Are you advanced in the science of the soul? Have you manifested your own soul above matter?" If he has not, then I say to him, "Religion has not come to you; it is all talk and book and vanity." But this poor Hindu sits before that idol and tries to think that he is That, and then says, "O Lord, I cannot conceive Thee as spirit, so let me conceive of Thee in this form"; and then he opens his eyes and see this form, and prostrating himself he repeats his prayers. And when his prayer is ended, he says, "O Lord, forgive me for this imperfect worship of Thee."

You are always being told that the Hindu worships blocks of stone. Now what do you think of this fervent nature of the souls of these people? I am the first monk to come over to these Western countries — it is the first time in the history of the world that a Hindu monk has crossed the ocean. But we hear such criticism and hear of these talks, and what is the general attitude of my nation towards you? They smile and say, "They are children;

they may be great in physical science; they may build huge things; but in religion they are simply children." That is the attitude of my people.

One thing I would tell you, and I do not mean any unkind criticism. You train and educate and clothe and pay men to do what? To come over to my country to curse and abuse all my forefathers, my religion, and everything. They walk near a temple and say, "You idolaters, you will go to hell." But they dare not do that to the Mohammedans of India; the sword would be out. But the Hindu is too mild; he smiles and passes on, and says, "Let the fools talk." That is the attitude. And then you who train men to abuse and criticise, if I just touch you with the least bit of criticism, with the kindest of purpose, you shrink and cry, "Don't touch us; we are Americans. We criticise all the people in the world, curse them and abuse them, say anything; but do not touch us; we are sensitive plants." You may do whatever you please; but at the same time I am going to tell you that we are content to live as we are; and in one thing we are better off — we never teach our children to swallow such horrible stuff: "Where every prospect pleases and man alone is vile." And whenever your ministers criticise us, let them remember this: If all India stands up and takes all the mud that is at the bottom of the Indian Ocean and throws it up against the Western countries, it will not be doing an infinitesimal part of that which you are doing to us. And what for? Did we ever send one missionary to convert anybody in the world? We say to you, "Welcome to your religion, but allow me to have mine." You call yours an aggressive religion. You are aggressive, but how many have you taken? Every sixth man in the world is a Chinese subject, a Buddhist; then there are Japan, Tibet, and Russia, and Siberia, and Burma, and Siam; and it may not be palatable, but this Christian morality, the Catholic Church, is all derived from them. Well, and how was this done? Without the shedding of one drop of blood! With all your brags and boastings, where has your Christianity succeeded without the sword? Show me one place in the whole world. One, I say, throughout the history of the Christian religion — one; I do not want two. I know how your forefathers were converted. They had to be converted or killed; that was all. What can you do better than Mohammedanism, with all your bragging? "We are the only one!" And why? "Because we can kill others." The Arabs said that; they bragged. And where is the Arab now? He is the bedouin. The Romans used to say that, and where are they now? Blessed are the peace-makers; they shall enjoy the earth. Such things tumble down; it is built upon sands; it cannot remain long.

Everything that has selfishness for its basis, competition as its right hand, and enjoyment as its goal, must die sooner or later. Such things must die. Let me tell you, brethren, if you want to live, if you really want your nation to live, go back to Christ. You are not Christians. No, as a nation you are not. Go back to Christ. Go back to him who had nowhere to lay his head. "The birds have their nests and the beasts their lairs, but the Son of Man has nowhere to lay his head." Yours is religion preached in the name of luxury. What an irony of fate! Reverse this if you want to live, reverse this. It is all hypocrisy that I have heard in this country. If this nation is going to live, let it go back to him. You cannot serve God and Mammon at the same time. All this prosperity, all this from Christ! Christ would have denied all such heresies. All prosperity which comes with Mammon is transient, is only for a moment. Real permanence is in Him. If you can join these two, this wonderful prosperity with the ideal of Christ, it is well. But if you cannot, better go back to him and give this up. Better be ready to live in rags with Christ than to live in palaces without him.

Christianity In India

(A lecture delivered at Detroit on March 11, 1894 and reported Detroit Free Press)

"Vive Kananda spoke to a crowded audience at the Detroit Opera House last night. He was given an extremely cordial reception and delivered his most eloquent address here. He spoke for two hours and a half.

Hon. T. W. Palmer, in introducing the distinguished visitor, referred to the old tale of the shield that was copper on one side and silver on the other and the contest which ensued. If we look on both sides of a question there would be less dispute. It is possible for all men to agree. The matter of foreign missions has been dear to the religious heart. Vive Kananda, from the Christian standpoint, said Mr. Palmer, was a pagan. It would be pleasant to hear from a gentleman who spoke about the copper side of the shield.

Vive Kananda was received with great applause." . . .

I do not know much about missionaries in Japan and China, but I am well posted about India. The people of this country look upon India as a vast waste, with many jungles and a few civilised Englishmen. India is half as large as the United States, and there are three hundred million people. Many stories are related, and I have become tired of denying these. The first invaders of India, the Aryans, did not try to exterminate the population of India as the Christians did when they went into a new land, but the endeavour was made to elevate persons of brutish habits. The Spaniards came to Ceylon with Christianity. The Spaniards thought that their God commanded them to kill and murder and to tear down heathen temples. The Buddhists had a tooth a foot long, which belonged to their Prophet, and the Spaniards threw it into the sea, killed a few thousand persons, and converted a few scores. The Portuguese came to Western India. The Hindus have a belief in the Trinity and had a temple dedicated to their sacred belief. The invaders looked at the temple and said it was a creation of the devil; and so they brought their cannon to bear upon the wonderful structure and destroyed a portion of it. But the invaders were driven out of the country by the enraged population. The early missionaries tried to get hold of the land, and in their effort to secure a foothold by force, they killed many people and converted a number. Some of them became Christians to save their lives. Ninety-nine percent of the Christians converted by the Portuguese sword were compelled to be so, and they said, "We do not believe in Christianity, but we are forced to call ourselves Christians." But Catholic Christianity soon relapsed.

The East India Company got possession of a part of India with the idea of making hay while the sun shone. They kept the missionaries away. The Hindus were the first to welcome the missionaries, not the Englishmen, who were engaged in trade. I have great admiration for some of the first missionaries of the later period, who were true servants of Jesus and did not vilify the people or spread vile falsehoods about them. They were gentle, kindly men. When Englishmen became masters of India, the missionary enterprise began to become stagnant, a condition which characterises the missionary efforts in India today. Dr. Long, an early missionary, stood by the people. He translated a Hindu drama describing the evils perpetuated in India by indigo-planters, and what was the result? He was placed in jail by the English. Such missionaries were of benefit to the country, but they have passed away. The Suez Canal opened up a number of evils.

Now goes the missionary, a married man, who is hampered because he is married. The missionary knows nothing about the people, he cannot speak the language, so he invariably settles in the little white colony. He is forced to do this because he is married. Were he not married, he could go among the people and sleep on the ground if necessary. So he goes to India to seek company for his wife and children. He stays among the English-speaking people. The great heart of India is today absolutely untouched by missionary effort. Most of the missionaries are incompetent. I have not met a single missionary who understands Sanskrit. How can a man absolutely ignorant of the people and their traditions, get into sympathy with them? I do not mean any offense, but Christians send men as missionaries, who are not persons of ability. It is sad to see money spent to make converts when no real results of a satisfactory nature are reached.

Those who are converted, are the few who make a sort of living by hanging round the missionaries. The converts who are not kept in service in India, cease to be converts. That is about the entire matter in a nutshell. As to the way of converting, it is absolutely absurd. The money the missionaries bring is accepted. The colleges founded by missionaries are all right, so far as the education is concerned. But with religion it is different. The Hindu is acute; he takes the bait but avoids the hook! It is wonderful how tolerant the people are. A missionary once said, "That is the worst of the whole business. People who are self-complacent can never be converted."

As regards the lady missionaries, they go into certain houses, get four shillings a month, teach them something of the Bible, and show them how to knit. The girls of India will never be converted. Atheism and skepticism at home is what is pushing the missionary into other lands. When I came into this country I was surprised to meet so many liberal men and women. But after the Parliament of Religions a great Presbyterian paper came out and gave me the benefit of a seething article. This the editor called enthusiasm. The missionaries do not and cannot throw off nationality — they are not broad enough — and so they accomplish nothing in the way of converting, although they may have a nice sociable time among themselves. India requires help from Christ, but not from the antichrist; these men are not Christlike. They do not act like Christ; they are married and come over and settle down comfortably and make a fair livelihood. Christ and his disciples would accomplish much good in India, just as many of the Hindu saints do; but these men are not of that sacred character. The Hindus would welcome the Christ of the Christians gladly, because his life was holy and beautiful; but they cannot and will not receive the narrow utterances of the ignorant, hypocritical or self-deceiving men.

Men are different. If they were not, the mentality of the world would be degraded. If there were not different religions, no religion would survive. The Christian requires his religion; the Hindu needs his own creed. All religions have struggled against one another for years. Those which were founded on a book, still stand. Why could not the Christians convert the Jews? Why could they not make the Persians Christians? Why could they not convert Mohammedans? Why cannot any impression be made upon China or Japan? Buddhism, the first missionary religion, numbers double the number of converts of any other religion, and they did not use the sword. The Mohammedans used the greatest violence. They number the least of the three great missionary religions. The Mohammedans have had their day. Every day you read of Christian nations acquiring land by bloodshed. What missionaries preach against this? Why should the most blood-thirsty nation exalt an alleged religion which is not the religion of Christ? The Jews and the Arabs were the fathers of Christianity, and how they have been persecuted by the Christians! The Christians have been weighed in the balance in India and have been found wanting. I do not mean to be unkind, but I want to show the Christians how they look in others' eyes. The missionaries who preach the burning pit are regarded with horror. The Mohammedans rolled wave after wave over India waving the sword, and today where are they?

The furthest that all religions can see is the existence of a spiritual entity. So no religion can teach beyond that point. In every religion there is the essential truth and the non-essential casket in which this jewel lies. Believing in the Jewish book or in the Hindu book is non-essential. Circumstances change; the receptacle is different; but the central truth remains. The essentials being the same, the educated people of every community retain the essentials. If you ask a Christian what his essentials are, he should reply, "The teachings of Lord Jesus." Much of the rest is nonsense. But the nonsensical part is right; it forms the receptacle. The shell of the oyster is not attractive, but the pearl is within it. The Hindu will never attack the life of Jesus; he reverences the Sermon on the Mount. But how many Christians know or have heard of the teachings of the Hindu holy men? They remain in a fool's paradise. Before a small fraction of the world was converted, Christianity was divided into many creeds. That is the law of nature. Why take a single instrument from the great religious orchestra of the earth? Let the grand symphony go on. Be pure. Give up superstition and see the wonderful harmony of nature. Superstition gets the better of religion. All the religions are good, since the essentials are the same. Each man should have the perfect exercise of his individuality, but these individualities form a perfect whole. This marvelous condition is already in existence. Each creed has something to add to the wonderful structure.

I pity the Hindu who does not see the beauty in Jesus Christ's character. I pity the Christian who does not reverence the Hindu Christ. The more a man sees of himself, the less he sees of his neighbors. Those that go about converting, who are very busy saving the souls of others, in many instances forget their own souls. I was asked by a lady why the women of India were not more elevated. It is in a great degree owing to the barbarous invaders through different ages; it is partly due to the people in India themselves. But our women are any day better than the ladies of this country who are devotees of novels and balls. Where is the spirituality one would expect in a country which is so boastful of its civilisation? I have not found it. "Here" and "here-after" are words to frighten children. It is all "here". To live and move in God — even here, even in this body! All self should go out; all superstition should be banished. Such men live in India. Where are such in this country? Your preachers speak against "dreamers". The people of this country would be better off if there were more "dreamers". If a man here followed literally the instruction of his Lord, he would be called a fanatic. There is a good deal of difference between dreaming and the brag of the nineteenth century. The bees look for the flowers. Open the lotus! The whole world is full of God and not of sin. Let us help each other. Let us love each other. A beautiful prayer of the Buddhist is: I bow down to all the saints; I bow down to all the prophets; I bow down to all the holy men and women all over the world!

The Religion Of Love

(Notes of a lecture delivered in London on November 16, 1895)

Just as it is necessary for a man to go through symbols and ceremonies first in order to arrive at the depth of realisation, so we say in India, "It is good to be born in a church, but bad to die in one". A sapling must be hedged about for protection, but when it becomes a tree, a hedge would be a hindrance. So there is no need to criticise and condemn the old forms. We forget that in religion there must be *growth*.

At first we think of a Personal God, and call Him Creator, Omnipotent, Omniscient, and so forth. But when loves comes, God is only love. The loving worshipper does not care *what* God is, because he wants nothing from Him. Says an Indian saint, "I am no beggar!" Neither does he fear. God is loved as a human being.

Here are some of the systems founded on love. (1) Shânta, a common, peaceful love, with such thoughts as those of fatherhood and help; (2) Dâsya, the ideal of service; God as master or general or sovereign, giving punishments and rewards; (3) Vâtsalya, God as mother or child. In India the mother never punishes. In each of these stages, the worshipper forms an ideal of God and follows it. Then (4) Sakhya, God as friend. There is here no fear. There is also the feeling of equality and familiarity. There are some Hindus who worship God as friend and playmate. Next comes (5) Madhura, sweetest love, the love of husband and wife. Of this St. Teresa and the ecstatic saints have been examples. Amongst the Persians, God has been looked upon as the wife, amongst the Hindus as the husband. We may recall the great queen Mirâ Bâi, who preached that the Divine Spouse was all. Some carry this to such an extreme that to call God "mighty" or "father" seems to them blasphemy. The language of this worship is erotic. Some even use that of illicit passion. To this cycle belongs the story of Krishna and the Gopi-girls. All this probably seems to you to entail great degeneration on the worshipper. And so it does. Yet many great saints have been developed by it. And no human institution is beyond abuse. Would you cook nothing because there are beggars? Would you possess nothing because there are thieves? "O Beloved, one kiss of Thy lips, once tasted, hath made me mad!"

The fruit of this idea is that one can no longer belong to any sect, or endure ceremonial. Religion in India culminates in freedom. But even this comes to be given up, and all is love for love's sake.

Last of all comes *love without distinction,* the Self. There is a Persian poem that tells how a lover came to the door of his beloved, and knocked. She asked, "Who art thou?" and he replied, "I am so and so, thy beloved!" and she answered only, "Go! I know none such!" But when she had asked for the fourth time, he said, "I am thyself, O my Beloved, therefore open thou to me!" And the door was opened.

A great saint said, using the language of a girl, describing love: "Four eyes met. There were changes in two souls. And now I cannot tell whether he is a man and I am a woman, or he is a woman and I a man. This only I remember, two souls were. Love came, and there was one."

In the highest love, union is only of the spirit. All love of any other kind is quickly evanescent. Only the spiritual lasts, and this grows.

Love sees the Ideal. This is the third angle of the triangle. God has been Cause, Creator, Father. Love is the culmination. The mother regrets that her child is humpbacked, but when she has nursed him for a few days, she loves him and thinks him most beautiful. The lover sees the beauty of Helen in the brow of Ethiopia. We do not commonly realise what happens. The brow of Ethiopia is merely a suggestion: the man *sees* Helen. His ideal is thrown upon the suggestion and covers it, as the oyster makes sand into a pearl. God is this ideal, through which man may see all.

Hence we come to love love itself. This love cannot be expressed. No words can utter it. We are dumb about it.

The senses become very much heightened in love. Human love, we must remember, is mixed up with attributes. It is dependent, too, on the other's attitude. Indian languages have words to describe this interdependence of love. The lowest love is selfish; it consists in pleasure of being loved. We say in India, "One gives the cheek, the other kisses." Above this is mutual love. But this also ceases mutually. True love is all giving. We do not even want to see the other, or to do anything to express our feeling. It is enough to give. It is almost impossible to love a human being like this, but it is possible to love God.

In India there is no idea of blasphemy if boys fighting in the street use the name of God. We say, "Put your hand into the fire, and whether you feel it or not, you will be burnt. So to utter the name of God can bring nothing but good."

The notion of blasphemy comes from the Jews, who were impressed by the spectacle of Persian loyalty. The ideas that God is judge and punisher are not in themselves bad, but they are low and vulgar. The three angles of the triangle are: Love begs not; Love knows no fear; Love is always the ideal.

"Who would be able to live one second,
Who would be able to breathe one moment,
If the Loving one had not filled the universe?"

Most of us will find that we were born for service. We must leave the results to God. The work was done only for love of God. If failure comes, there need be no sorrow. The work was done only for love of God.

In women, the mother-nature is much developed. They worship God as the child. They ask nothing, and will do anything.

The Catholic Church teaches many of these deep things, and though it is narrow, it is religious in the highest sense. In modern society, Protestantism is broad but shallow. To judge truth by what good it does is as bad as to question the value of a scientific discovery to a baby.

Society must be outgrown. We must crush law and become outlaws. We allow nature, only in order to conquer her. Renunciation means that none can serve both God and Mammon.

Deepen your own power of thought and love. Bring your own lotus to blossom: the bees will come of themselves. Believe first in yourself, then in God. A handful of strong men will move the world. We need a heart to feel, a brain to conceive, and a strong arm to do the work. Buddha gave himself for the animals. Make yourself a fit agent to work. But it is God who works, not you. One man contains the whole universe. One particle of matter has all the energy of the universe at its back. In a conflict between the heart and the brain follow your heart.

Yesterday, competition was the law. Today, cooperation is the law. Tomorrow there is no law. Let sages praise thee, or let the world blame. Let fortune itself come, or let poverty and rags stare thee in the face. Eat the herbs of the forest, one day, for food; and the next, share a banquet of fifty courses. Looking neither to right hand nor to the left, follow thou on!

The Swami began by telling, in answer to questions, the story of how Pavhâri Bâbâ snatched up his own vessels and ran after the thief, only to fall at his feet and say:

"O Lord, I knew not that Thou wert there! Take them! They are Thine! Pardon me, Thy child!"

Again he told how the same saint was bitten by a cobra, and when, towards nightfall he recovered, he said, "A messenger came to me from the Beloved."

Jnana And Karma

*(Notes of a lecture delivered in London,
on November 23, 1895)*

The greatest force is derived from the power of thought. *The finer the element, the more powerful it is.* The silent power of thought influences people even at a distance, because mind is one as well as many. The universe is a cobweb; minds are spiders.

The universe equals the phenomena of one Universal Being. He, seen through our senses, is the universe. This is Maya. So the world is illusion, that is, the imperfect vision of the Real, a semi-revelation, even as the sun in the morning is a red ball. Thus all evils and wickedness are but weakness, the *imperfect vision of goodness.*

A straight line projected infinitely becomes a circle. The search for good comes back to Self. I am the whole mystery, God. I am a body, the lower self; and I am the Lord of the universe.

Why should a man be moral and pure? Because this strengthens his will. Everything that strengthens the will by revealing the real nature is moral. Everything that does the reverse is immoral. The standard varies from country to country, from individual to individual. Man must recover from his state of slavery to laws, to words, and so on. We have no freedom of the will now, but we shall have when we are free. Renunciation is this giving up of the world. Through the senses, anger comes, and sorrow comes. As long as renunciation is not *there,* self and the passion animating it are different. At last they become identified, and the man is an animal at once. Become possessed with the feeling of renunciation.

I once had a body, was born, struggled and died: What [illegible] hallucinations! To think that one was cramped in a body, w[illegible] salvation!

But does renunciation demand that we all become ascetics? Who then is to help others? Renunciation is not asceticism. Are all beggars Christ? Poverty is not a synonym for holiness; often the reverse. Renunciation is of the mind. How does it come? In a desert, when I was thirsty, I saw a lake. It was in the midst of a beautiful landscape. There were trees surrounding it, and their reflections could be seen in the water, upside down. But the whole thing proved to be a mirage. Then I knew that every day for a month I had seen this; and only that day, being thirsty, I had learnt it to be unreal. Every day for a month I should see it again. But I should never take it to be real. So, when we reach God, the idea of the universe, the body and so on, will vanish. It will return afterwards. But next time we shall know it to be unreal.

The history of the world is the history of persons like Buddha and Jesus. The passionless and unattached do most for the world. Picture Jesus in the slums. He sees beyond the misery, "You, my brethren, are all divine." His work is calm. He removes causes. You will be able to work for the good of the world when you know for a fact that this work is all illusion. The more unconscious this work, the better, because it is then the more superconscious. Our search is not for good or evil; but happiness and good are nearer to truth than their opposites. A man ran a thorn into his finger, and with another thorn took it out. The first thorn is Evil. The second thorn is Good. The Self is that Peace which passeth beyond both evil and good. The universe is melting down: man draws nearer to God. For one moment he is real — God. He is re-differentiated — a prophet. Before him, now, the world trembles. A fool sleeps and wakes a fool-a man unconscious; and superconscious, he returns with infinite power, purity, and love — the God-Man. This is the use of the superconscious state.

Wisdom can be practised even on a battlefield. The Gitâ was preached so. There are three states of mind: the active, the passive, and the serene. The passive state is characterised by slow vibrations; the active by quick vibrations, and the serene by the most intense vibrations of all. Know that the soul is sitting in the chariot. The body is the chariot; the outer senses are the horses; and the mind the reins; and the intellect the charioteer. So man crosses the ocean of Maya. He goes beyond. He reaches God. When a man is under the control of his senses, he is of this world. When he has controlled the senses, he has renounced.

Even forgiveness, if weak and passive, is not true: fight is better. *Forgive* when you could bring legions of angels to the victory. Krishna, the charioteer of Arjuna, hears him say, "Let us forgive our enemies", and answers, "You speak the words of wise men, but you are not a wise man, but a coward". As a lotus-leaf, living in the water yet untouched by it, so should the soul be in the world. This is a battlefield, fight your way out. Life in this world is an attempt to see God. Make your life a manifestation of will strengthened by renunciation.

We must learn to control all our brain-centres consciously. The first step is the joy of living. Asceticism is fiendish. To laugh is better than to pray.

Sing. Get rid of misery. Do not for heaven's sake infect others with it. Never think God sells a little happiness and a little unhappiness. Surround yourself with flowers and pictures and incense. The saints went to the mountain tops to enjoy nature.

The second step is purity.

The third is full training of the mind. Reason out what is true from what is untrue. See that God alone is true. If for a moment you think you are not God, great terror will seize you. As soon as you think "*I am He*", great peace and joy will come to you. Control the senses. If a man curses me, I should still see in him God, whom through my weakness I see as a curser. The poor man to whom you do good is extending a privilege to you. He allows you, through His mercy, to worship Him thus.

The history of the world is the history of a few men who had faith in themselves. That faith calls out the divinity within. You can do anything. You fail only when you do not strive sufficiently to manifest infinite power. As soon as a man or a nation loses faith, death comes.

There is a divine within that cannot be overcome either by church dogmas or by blackguardism. A handful of Greeks speak wherever there is civilisation. Some mistakes there must always be. Do not grieve. Have great insight. Do *not* think, "What is done is done. Oh, that 'twere done better!" If man had not been God, humanity would by this time have become insane, with its litanies and its penitence.

None will be left, none destroyed. All will in the end be made perfect. Say, day and night, "Come up, my brothers! You are the infinite ocean of purity! Be God! Manifest as God!"

What is civilisation? It is the feeling of the divine within. When you find time, repeat these ideas to yourself and desire freedom. That is all. Deny everything that is not God. Assert everything that is God. Mentally assert this, day and night. So the veil grows thinner:

"I am neither man nor angel. I have no sex nor limit. I am knowledge itself. I am He. I have neither anger nor hatred. I have neither pain nor pleasure. Death or birth I never had. For I am Knowledge Absolute, and Bliss Absolute. I am He, my soul, I am He!"

Find yourself bodiless. You never had a body. It was all superstition. Give back the divine consciousness to all the poor, the downtrodden, the oppressed, and the sick.

Apparently, every five hundred years or so, a wave of this thought comes over the world. Little waves arise in many directions: but one swallows up all the others and sweeps over society. That wave does this which has most character at its back.

Confucius, Moses, and Pythagoras; Buddha, Christ, Mohammed; Luther, Calvin, and the Sikhs; Theosophy, Spiritualism, and the like; all these mean only the preaching of the Divine-in-Man.

Never say man is weak. Wisdom-Yoga is no better than the others. Love is the ideal and requires no object. Love is God. So even through devotion we reach the subjective God. I am He! How can one work, unless one loves city, country, animals, the universe? Reason leads to the finding of unity in variety. Let the atheist and the agnostic work for the social good. So God comes.

But this you must guard against: Do not disturb the faith of any. For you must know that religion is not in doctrines. Religion lies in being and becoming, in realisation. All men are born idolaters. The lowest man is an animal. The highest man is perfect. And between these two, all have to think in sound and colour, in doctrine and ritual.

The test of having ceased to be an idolater is: "When you say 'I', does the body come into your thought or not? If it does, then you are still a worshipper of idols." Religion is not intellectual jargon at all, but realisation. If you *think* about God, you are only a fool. The ignorant man, by prayer and devotion, can reach beyond the philosopher. To know God, no philosophy is necessary. Our duty is not to disturb the faith of others. Religion is experience. Above all and in all, be sincere; identification brings misery, because it brings desire. Thus the poor man sees gold, and identifies himself with the need of gold. Be the witness. *Learn never to react.*

The Claims Of Vedanta On The Modern World

(Report of a lecture delivered in Oakland on Sunday, February 25, 1900, with editorial comments of the Oakland Enquirer)

The announcement that Swami Vivekananda, a distinguished savant of the East, would expound the philosophy of Vedanta in the Parliament of Religions at the Unitarian Church last evening, attracted an immense throng. The main auditorium and ante-rooms were packed, the annexed auditorium of Wendte Hall was thrown open, and this was also filled to overflowing, and it is estimated that fully 500 persons, who could not obtain seats or standing room where they could hear conveniently, were turned away.

The Swami created a marked impression. Frequently he received applause during the lecture, and upon concluding, held a levee of enthusiastic admirers. He said in part, under the subject of "The Claims of Vedanta on the Modern World":

Vedanta demands the consideration of the modern world. The largest number of the human race is under its influence. Again and again, millions upon millions have swept down on its adherents in India, crushing them with their great force, and yet the religion lives.

In all the nations of the world, can such a system be found? Others have risen to come under its shadow. Born like mushrooms, today they are alive and flourishing, and tomorrow they are gone. Is this not the survival of the fittest?

It is a system not yet complete. It has been growing for thousands of years and is still growing. So I can give you but an idea of all I would say in one brief hour.

First, to tell you of the history of the rise of Vedanta. When it arose, India had already perfected a religion. Its crystallisation had been going on many years. Already there were elaborate ceremonies; already there had been perfected a system of morals for the different stages of life. But there came a rebellion against the mummeries and mockeries that enter into many religions in time, and great men came forth to proclaim through the

Vedas the true religion. Hindus received their religion from the revelation of these Vedas. They were told that the Vedas were without beginning and without end. It may sound ludicrous to this audience — how a book can be without beginning or end; but by the Vedas no books are meant. They mean the accumulated treasury of spiritual laws discovered by different persons in different times.

Before these men came, the popular ideas of a God ruling the universe, and that man was immortal, were in existence. But there they stopped. It was thought that nothing more could be known. Here came the daring of the expounders of Vedanta. They knew that religion meant for children is not good for thinking men; that there is something more to man and God.

The moral agnostic knows only the external dead nature. From that he would form the law of the universe. He might as well cut off my nose and claim to form an idea of my whole body, as argue thus. He must look within. The stars that sweep through the heavens, even the universe is but a drop in the bucket. Your agnostic sees not the greatest, and he is frightened at the universe.

The world of spirit is greater than all — the God of the universe who rules — our Father, our Mother. What is this heathen mummery we call the world? There is misery everywhere. The child is born with a cry upon its lips; it is its first utterance. This child becomes a man, and so well used to misery that the pang of the heart is hidden by a smile on the lips.

Where is the solution of this world? Those who look outside will never find it; they must turn their eyes inward and find truth. Religion lives inside.

One man preaches, if you chop your head off, you get salvation. But does he get any one to follow him? Your own Jesus says, "Give all to the poor and follow me." How many of you have done this? You have not followed out this command, and yet Jesus was the great teacher of your religion. Every one of you is practical in his own life, and you find this would be impracticable.

But Vedanta offers you nothing that is impracticable. Every science must have its own matter to work upon. Everyone needs certain conditions and much of training and learning; but any Jack in the street can tell you all about religion. You may want to follow religion and follow an expert, but you may only care to converse with Jack, for he can talk it.

You must do with religion as with science, come in direct contact with facts, and on that foundation build a marvellous structure.

To have a true religion you must have instruments. Belief is not in question; of faith you can make nothing, for you can believe anything.

We know that in science as we increase the velocity, the mass decreases; and as we increase the mass, the velocity decreases. Thus we have matter and force. The matter, we do not know how, disappears into force, and force into matter. Therefore there is something which is neither force nor matter, as these two may not disappear into each other. This is what we call mind — the universal mind.

Your body and my body are separate, you say. I am but a little whirlpool in the universal ocean of mankind. A whirlpool, it is true, but a part of the great ocean.

You stand by moving water where every particle is changing, and yet you call it a stream. The water is changing, it is true, but the banks remain the same. The mind is not changing, but the body — how quick its growth! I was a baby, a boy, a man, and soon I will be an old man, stooped and aged. The body is changing, and you say, is the mind not changing also? When I was a child, I was thinking, I have become larger, because my mind is a sea of impressions.

There is behind nature a universal mind. The spirit is simply a unit and it is not matter. For man is a spirit. The question, "Where does the soul go after death?" should be answered like the boy when he asked, "Why does not the earth fall down?" The questions are alike, and their solutions alike; for where could the soul go to?

To you who talk of immortality I would ask when you go home to endeavour to imagine you are dead. Stand by and touch your dead body. You cannot, for you cannot get out of yourself. The question is not concerning immortality, but as to whether Jack will meet his Jenny after death.

The one great secret of religion is to know for yourself that you are a spirit. Do not cry out, "I am a worm, I am nobody!" As the poet says, "I am Existence, Knowledge, and Truth." No man can do any good in the world by crying out, "I am one of its evils." The more perfect, the less imperfections you see.

The Laws Of Life And Death

(Report of a lecture delivered in Oakland on March 7, 1900, with editorial comments of the Oakland Tribune)

Swami Vivekananda delivered a lecture last evening on the subject, "The Laws of Life and Death". The Swami said: "How to get rid of this birth and death — not how to go to heaven, but how one can stop going to heaven — this is the object of the search of the Hindu."

The Swami went on to say that nothing stands isolated — everything is a part of the never-ending procession of cause and effect. If there are higher beings than man, they also must obey the laws. Life can only spring from life, thought from thought, matter from matter. A universe cannot be created out of matter. It has existed for ever. If human beings came into the world fresh from the hands of nature, they would come without impressions; but we do not come in that way, which shows that we are not created afresh. If human souls are created out of nothing, what is to prevent them from going back into nothing? If we are to live all the time in the future, we must have lived all the time in the past.

It is the belief of the Hindu that the soul is neither mind nor body. What is it which remains stable — which can say, "I am I"? Not the body, for it is always changing; and not the mind, which changes more rapidly than the body, which never has the same thoughts for even a few minutes. There must be an identity which does not change — something which is to man what the banks are to the river — the banks which do not change and without whose immobility we would not be conscious of the constantly moving stream. Behind the body, behind the mind, there must be something, viz the soul, which unifies the man. Mind is merely the fine instrument through which the soul — the master — acts on the body. In India we say a man has given up his body, while you say, a man gives up his ghost. The Hindus believe that a man is a soul and has a body, while Western people believe he is a body and possesses a soul.

Death overtakes everything which is complex. The soul is a single element, not composed of anything else, and therefore it cannot die. By its very nature the soul must be immortal. Body, mind, and soul turn upon the wheel of law — none can escape. No more can we transcend the law than can the stars, than can the sun — it is all a universe of law. The law of Karma is that every action must be followed sooner or later by an effect. The Egyptian seed which was taken from the hand of a mummy after 5000 years and sprang into life when planted is the type of the never-ending influence of human acts. Action can never die without producing action. Now, if our acts can only produce their appropriate effects on this plane of existence, it follows that we must all come back to round out the circle of causes and effects. This is the doctrine of reincarnation. We are the slaves of law, the slaves of conduct, the slaves of thirst, the slaves of desire, the slaves of a thousand things. Only by escaping from life can we escape from slavery to freedom. God is the only one who is free. God and freedom are one and the same.

The Reality And The Shadow

(Report of a lecture delivered in Oakland on March 8, 1900, with editorial comments of the Oakland Tribune)

Swami Vivekananda, the Hindu philosopher, delivered another lecture in Wendte Hall last evening. His subject was: "The Reality and The Shadow". He said:

"The soul of man is ever striving after certainty, to find something that does not change. It is never satisfied. Wealth, the gratification of ambition or of appetite are all changeable. Once these are attained, man is not content. Religion is the science which teaches us whence to satisfy this longing after the unchangeable. Behind all the local colours and derivations they teach the same thing — that there is reality only in the soul of man.

"The philosophy of Vedanta teaches that there are two worlds, the external or sensory, and the internal or subjective — the thought world.

"It posits three fundamental concepts — time, space, and causation. From these is constituted Mâyâ, the essential groundwork of human thought, not the product of thought. This same conclusion was arrived at a later date by the great German philosopher Kant.

"My reality, that of nature and of God, is the same, the difference is in form of manifestation. The differentiation is caused by Maya. The contour of the shore may shape the ocean into bay, strait, or inlet; but when this shaping force or Maya is removed, the separate form disappears, the differentiation ceases, all is ocean again."

The Swami then spoke of the roots of the theory of evolution to be found in the Vedanta philosophy.

All modern religions start with the idea," continued the speaker, "that man was once pure, he fell, and will become pure again. I do not see where they get this idea. The seat of knowledge is the soul; external circumstance simply stimulates the soul; knowledge is the power of the soul. Century after century it has been manufacturing bodies. The various forms of incarnation are merely successive chapters of the story of the life of the soul. We are constantly building our bodies. The whole universe is in a state of flux, of expansion and contraction, of change. Vedanta holds that the soul never changes in essence, but it is modified by Maya. Nature is God limited by mind. The evolution of nature is the modification of the soul. The soul in essence is the same in all forms of being. Its expression is modified by the body. This unity of soul, this common substance of humanity, is the basis of ethics and morality. In this sense all are one, and to hurt one's brother is to hurt one's Self.

"Love is simply an expression of this infinite unity. Upon what dualistic system can you explain love? One of the European philosophers says that kissing is a survival of cannibalism, a kind of expression of 'how good you taste'. I do not believe it.

"What is it we all seek? Freedom. All the effort and struggle of life is for freedom. It is the march universal of races, of worlds, and of systems.

"If we are bound, who bound us? No power can bind the Infinite but Itself."

After the discourse an opportunity was afforded for asking questions of the speaker, who devoted half an hour to answering them.

Way To Salvation

(Report of a lecture delivered in Oakland on Monday, March 12, 1900, with editorial comments of the Oakland Enquirer)

Wendte Hall of the First Unitarian Church was crowded last evening with a large audience to hear the "Way to Salvation" from the standpoint of the Hindu priest, Swami Vivekananda. This was the last lecture of a series of three which the Swami has delivered. He said in part:

One man says God is in heaven, another that God is in nature and everywhere present. But when the great crisis comes, we find the goal is the same. We all work on different plans, but the end is not different.

The two great watchwords of every great religion are renunciation and self-sacrifice. We all want the truth, and we know that it must come, whether we want it or not. In a way we are all striving for that good. And what prevents our reaching it? It is ourselves. Your ancestors used to call it the devil; but it is our own false self.

We live in slavery, and we would die if we were out of it. We are like the man who lived in total darkness for ninety years and when taken out into the warm sunshine of nature, prayed to be taken back to his dungeon. You would not leave this old life to go into a newer and greater freedom which opens out.

The great difficulty is to go to the heart of things. These little degraded delusions of Jack So-and-So's, who thinks he has an infinite soul, however small he is with his different religions. In one country, all as a matter of religion, a man has many wives; in another one woman has many husbands. So some men have two gods, some one God, and some no God at all.

But salvation is in work and love. You learn something thoroughly; in time you may not be able to call that thing to memory. Yet it has sunk into your inner consciousness and is a part of you. So as you work, whether it be good or bad, you shape your future course of life. If you do good work with the idea of work — work for work's sake — you will go to heaven of your idea and dream of heaven.

The history of the world is not of its great men, of its demi-gods, but it is the little islands of the sea, which build themselves to great continents from fragments of the sea drift. Then the history of the world is in the little acts of sacrifice performed in every household. Man accepts religion because he does not wish to stand on his own judgment. He takes it as the best way of getting out of a bad place.

The salvation of man lies in the great love with which he loves his God. Your wife says, "O John, I could not live without you." Some men when they lose their money have to be sent to the asylum. Do you feel that way about your God? When you can give up money, friends, fathers and mothers, brothers and sisters, all that is in the world and only pray to God that He grant you something of His love, then you have found salvation.

The People Of India

(Report of a lecture delivered in Oakland on Monday, March 19, 1900, with editorial comments of the Oakland Enquirer)

The lecture which the Swami Vivekananda gave Monday night in his new course on "The People of India", was interesting, not only for what he had to relate of the people of that country, but for the insight into their mental attitude and prejudices which the speaker gave without really meaning it. It is apparent that the Swami, educated and intellectual man that he is, is no admirer of Western civilisation. He has evidently been a good deal embittered by the talk about child widows, the oppression of women, and other barbarisms alleged against the people of India, and is somewhat inclined to resort to the *tu quoque* in reply.

In commencing his talk, he gave his hearers an idea of the racial characteristics of the people. He said that the bond of unity in India, as in other countries of Asia, is not language or race, but religion. In Europe the race makes the nation, but in Asia people of diverse origin and different tongues become one nation if they have the same religion. The people of Northern India are divided into four great classes, while in Southern India the languages are so entirely different from those of Northern India that there is no kinship whatever. The people of Northern India belong to the great Aryan race, to which all of the people of Europe, except the Basques in the Pyrennees, and the Finns, are supposed to belong. The Southern India people belong to the same race as the ancient Egyptians and the Semites. To illustrate the difficulties of learning one another's languages in India, the Swami said that when he had occasion to go into Southern India, he always talked with the native people in English, unless they belonged to the select few who could speak Sanskrit.

A good deal of the lecture was taken up in a discussion of the caste system which the Swami characterised by saying that it had its bad side, but that its benefits outweighed its disadvantages. In brief, this caste system had grown by the practice of the son always following the business of the father. In course of time the community came thus to be divided into a series of classes, each held rigidly within its own boundaries. But while this divided the people, it also united them, because all the members of a caste were bound to help their fellows in case of need. And as no man could rise out of his caste, the Hindus have no such struggles for social or personal supremacy as embitter the people of other countries.

The worst feature of the caste is that is suppresses competition, and the checking of competition has really been the cause of the political downfall of India and its conquest by foreign races.

Respecting the much-discussed subject of marriage, the Hindus are socialistic and see nothing good in matches being made by a couple of young people who might be attached to one another, without regard to the welfare of the community, which is more important than that of any two persons. "Because I love Jennie and Jennie loves me", said the Swami, "is no reason why we should be married."

He denied that the condition of the child widows is as bad as has been represented, saying that in India the position of widows in general is one of a great deal of influence, because a large part of the property in the country is held by widows. In fact, so enviable is the position of widows that a woman or a man either might almost pray to be made a widow.

The child widows, or women who have been betrothed to children who died before marriage, might be pitied if a marriage were the only real object in life, but, according to the Hindu way of thinking, marriage is rather a duty than a privilege, and the denial of the right of child widows to marry is no particular hardship.

I Am That I Am

(Notes of a lecture give in San Francisco on March 20, 1900)

The subject tonight is man, man in contrast with nature. For a long time the word "nature" was used almost exclusively to denote external phenomena. These phenomena were found to behave methodically; and they often repeated themselves: that which had happened in the past happened again — nothing happened only once. Thus it was concluded that nature was uniform. Uniformity is closely associated with the idea of nature; without it natural phenomena cannot be understood. This uniformity is the basis of what we call law.

Gradually the word "nature" and the idea of uniformity came to be applied also to internal phenomena, the phenomena of life and mind. All that is differentiated is nature. Nature is the quality of the plant, the quality of the animal, and the quality of man. Man's life behaves according to definite methods; so does his mind. Thoughts do not just happen, there is a certain method in their rise, existence and fall. In other words, just as external phenomena are bound by law, internal phenomena, that is to say, the life and mind of man, are also bound by law.

When we consider law in relation to man's mind and existence, it is at once obvious that there can be no such thing as free will and free existence. We know how animal nature is wholly regulated by law. The animal does not appear to exercise any free will. The same is true of man; human nature also is bound by law. The law governing functions of the human mind is called the law of Karma.

Nobody has ever seen anything produced out of nothing; if anything arises in the mind, that also must have been produced from something. When we speak of free will, we mean the will is not caused by anything. But that cannot be true, the will is caused; and since it is caused, it cannot be free — it is bound by law. That I am willing to talk to you and you come to listen to me, that is law. Everything that I do or think or feel, every part of my conduct or behaviour, my every movement — all is caused and therefore not free. This regulation of our life and mind — that is the law of Karma.

If such a doctrine had been introduced in olden times into a Western community, it would have produced a tremendous commotion. The Western man does not want to think his mind is governed by law. In India it was accepted as soon as it was propounded by the most ancient Indian system of philosophy. There is no such thing as freedom of the mind; it cannot be. Why did not this teaching create any disturbance in the Indian mind? India received it calmly; that is the speciality of Indian thought, wherein it differs from every other thought in the world.

The external and internal natures are not two different things; they are really one. Nature is the sum total of all phenomena. "Nature" means all that is, all that moves. We make a tremendous distinction between matter and mind; we think that the mind is entirely different from matter. Actually, they are but one nature, half of which is continually acting on the other half. Matter is pressing upon the mind in the form of various sensations. These sensations are nothing but force. The force from the outside evokes the force within. From the will to respond to or get away from the outer force, the inner force becomes what we call thought.

Both matter and mind are really nothing but forces; and if you analyse them far enough, you will find that at root they are one. The very fact that the external force can somehow evoke the internal force shows that somewhere they join each other — they must be continuous and, therefore, basically the same force. When you get to the root of things, they become simple and general. Since the same force appears in one form as matter and in another form as mind, there is no reason to think matter and mind are different. Mind is changed into matter, matter is changed into mind. Thought force becomes nerve force, muscular force; muscular and nerve force become thought force. Nature is all this force, whether expressed as matter or mind.

The difference between the subtlest mind and the grossest matter is only one of degree. Therefore the whole universe may be called either mind or matter, it does not matter which. You may call the mind refined matter, or the body concretised mind; it makes little difference by which name you call which. All the troubles arising from the conflict between materialism and spirituality are due to wrong thinking. Actually, there is no difference between the two. I and the lowest pig differ only in degree. It is less manifested, I am more. Sometimes I am worse, the pig is better.

Nor is it any use discussing which comes first — mind or matter. Is the mind first, out of which matter has come? Or is matter first, out of which the mind has come? Many of the philosophical arguments proceed from these futile questions. It is like asking whether the egg or the hen is first. Both are first, and both last — mind and matter, matter and mind. If I say matter exists first and matter, growing finer and finer, becomes mind, then I must admit that before matter there must have been mind. Otherwise, where did matter come from? Matter precedes mind, mind precedes matter. It is the hen and the egg question all through.

The whole of nature is bound by the law of causation and is in time and space. We cannot see anything outside of space, yet we do not know space. We cannot perceive anything outside of time, yet we do not know time. We cannot understand anything except in terms of causality, yet we do not know what causation is. These three things — time, space, and causality — are in and through every phenomena, but they are not phenomena. They are as it were the forms or moulds in which everything must be cast before it can be apprehended. Matter is substance plus time, space, and causation. Mind is substance plus time, space and causation.

This fact can be expressed in another way. Everything is substance plus name and form. Name and form come and go, but substance remains ever the same. Substance, form, and name make this pitcher. When it is broken, you do not call it pitcher any more, nor do you see its pitcher form. Its name and form vanish, but its substance remains. All the differentiation in substance is made by name and form. There are not real, because they vanish. What we call nature is not the substance, unchanging and indestructible. Nature is time, space and causation. Nature is name and form. Nature is Mâyâ. Maya means name and form, into which everything is cast. Maya is not real. We could not destroy it or change it if it were real. The substance is the noumenon, Maya is phenomena. There is the real "me" which nothing can destroy, and there is the phenomenal "me" which is continually changing and disappearing.

The fact is, everything existing has two aspects. One is noumenal, unchanging and indestructible; the other is phenomenal, changing and destructible. Man in his true nature is substance, soul, spirit. This soul, this spirit, never changes, is never destroyed; but it appears to be clothed with a form and to have a name associated with it. This form and name are not immutable or indestructible; they continually change and are destroyed. Yet men foolishly seek immortality in this changeable aspect, in the body and mind — they want to have an eternal body. I do not want that kind of immortality.

What is the relation between me and nature? In so far as nature stands for name and form or for time, space, and causality, I am not part of nature, because I am free, I am immortal, I am unchanging and infinite. The question does not arise whether I have free will or not; I am beyond any will at all. Wherever there is will, it is never free. There is no freedom of will whatever. There is freedom of that which becomes will when name and form get hold of it, making it their slave. That substance — the soul — as it were moulds itself, as it were throws itself into the cast of name and form, and immediately becomes bound, whereas it was free before. And yet its original nature is still there. That is why it says, "I am free; in spite of all this bondage, I am free." And it never forgets this.

But when the soul has become the will, it is no more really free. Nature pulls the strings, and it has to dance as nature wants it to. Thus have you and I danced throughout the years. All the things that we see, do, feel, know, all our thoughts and actions, are nothing but dancing to the dictates of nature. There has been, and there is, no freedom in any of this. From the lowest to the highest, all thoughts and actions are bound by law, and none of these pertain to our real Self.

My true Self is beyond all law. Be in tune with slavery, with nature, and you live under law, you are happy under law. But the more you obey nature and its dictates, the more bound you become; the more in harmony with ignorance you are, the more you are at the beck and call of everything in the universe. Is this harmony with nature, this obedience to law, in accord with the true nature and destiny of man? What mineral ever quarrelled with and disputed any law? What tree or plant ever defied any law? This table is in harmony with nature, with law; but a table it remains always, it does not become any better. Man begins to struggle and fight against nature. He makes many mistakes, he suffers. But eventually he conquers nature and realises his freedom. When he is free, nature becomes his slave.

The awakening of the soul to its bondage and its effort to stand up and assert itself — this is called life. Success in this struggle is called evolution. The eventual triumph, when all the slavery is blown away, is called salvation, Nirvâna, freedom. Everything in the universe is struggling for liberty. When I am bound by nature, by name and form, by time, space and causality, I do not know what I truly am. But even in this bondage my real Self is not completely lost. I strain against the bonds; one by one they break, and I become conscious of my innate grandeur. Then comes complete liberation. I attain to the clearest and fullest consciousness of myself — I know that I am the infinite spirit, the master of nature, not its slave. Beyond all differentiation and combination, beyond space, time and causation, I am that I am.

Unity

(Notes of a lecture delivered at the Vedanta Society, New York, in June, 1900)

The different sectarian systems of India all radiate from one central idea of unity or dualism.

They are all under Vedanta, all interpreted by it. Their final essence is the teaching of unity. This, which we see as many, is God. We perceive matter, the world, manifold sensation. Yet there is but one existence.

These various names mark only differences of degree in the expression of that One. The worm of today is the God of tomorrow. These distinctions which we do love are all parts of one infinite fact, and only differ in the degree of expression. That one infinite fact is the attainment of freedom.

However mistaken we may be as to the method, all our struggle is really for freedom. We seek neither misery nor happiness, but freedom. This one aim is the secret of the insatiable thirst of man. Man's thirst, says the Hindu, man's thirst, says the Buddhist, is a burning, unquenchable thirst for more and more. You Americans are always looking for more pleasure, more enjoyment. You cannot be satisfied, true; but at bottom what you seek is freedom.

This vastness of his desire is really the sign of man's own infinitude. It is because he is infinite, that he can only be satisfied when his desire is infinite and its fulfilment infinite.

What then can satisfy man? Not gold. Not enjoyment. Not beauty. One Infinite alone can satisfy him, and that Infinite is Himself. When he realises this, then alone comes freedom.

> "This flute, with the sense-organs as its keyholes,
> With all its sensations, perceptions, and song,
> Is singing only one thing. It longs to go back to the
> wood whence it was cut!"
> "Deliver thou thyself by thyself!
> Ah, do not let thyself sink!

> For thou art thyself thy greatest friend.
> And thou thyself thy greatest enemy."

Who can help the Infinite? Even the hand that comes to you through the darkness will have to be your own.

Fear and desire are the two causes of all this, and who creates them? We ourselves. Our lives are but a passing from dream to dream. Man the infinite dreamer, dreaming finite dreams!

Oh, the blessedness of it, that nothing external can be eternal! They little know what they mean, whose hearts quake when they hear that nothing in this relative world can be eternal.

I am the infinite blue sky. Over me pass these clouds of various colours, remain a moment, and vanish. I am the same eternal blue. I am the witness, the same eternal witness of all. I see, therefore nature exists. I do not see, therefore she does not. Not one of us could see or speak if this infinite unity were broken for a moment.

The Worship Of The Divine Mother

(Fragmentary notes taken on a Sunday afternoon in New York in June, 1900)

From the tribal or clan-God, man arrives, in every religion, at the sum, the God of gods.

Confucius alone has expressed the one eternal idea of ethics. "Manu Deva" was transformed into Ahriman. In India, the mythological expression was suppressed; but the idea remained. In an old Veda is found the Mantra, "I am the empress of all that lives, the power in everything."

Mother-worship is a distinct philosophy in itself. Power is the first of our ideas. It impinges upon man at every step; power felt within is the soul; without, nature. And the battle between the two makes human life. All that we know or feel is but the resultant of these two forces. Man saw that the sun shines on the good and evil alike. Here was a new idea of God, as the Universal Power behind all — the Mother-idea was born.

Activity, according to Sânkhya, belongs to Prakriti, to nature, not to Purusha or soul. Of all feminine types in India, the mother is pre-eminent. The mother stands by her child through everything. Wife and children may desert a man, but his mother never! Mother, again, is the impartial energy of the universe, because of the colourless love that asks not, desires not, cares not for the evil in her child, but loves him the more. And today Mother-worship is the worship of all the highest classes amongst the Hindus.

The goal can only be described as something not yet attained. Here, there is no goal. This world is all alike the play of Mother. But we forget this. Even misery can be enjoyed when there is no selfishness, when we have become the witness of our own lives. The thinker of this philosophy has been struck by the idea that one *power* is behind all phenomena. In our thought of God, there is human limitation, personality: with Shakti comes the idea of One Universal Power. "I stretch the bow of Rudra when He desires to kill", says Shakti. The Upanisads did not develop this thought; for Vedanta does not care for the God-idea. But in the Gita comes the significant saying to Arjuna, "I am the real, and I am the unreal. I bring good, and I bring evil."

Again the idea slept. Later came the new philosophy. This universe is a composite fact of good and evil; and one Power must be manifesting through both. "A lame one-legged universe makes only a lame one-legged God." And this, in the end, lands us in want of sympathy and makes us brutal. The ethics built upon such a concept is an ethics of brutality. The saint hates the sinner, and the sinner struggles against the saint. Yet even this leads onward. For finally the wicked self-sufficient mind will die, crushed under repeated blows; and then we shall awake and know the Mother.

Eternal, unquestioning self-surrender to Mother alone can give us peace. Love Her for Herself, without fear or favour. Love Her because you are Her child. See Her in all, good and bad alike. Then alone will come "Sameness" and Bliss Eternal that is Mother Herself when we realise Her thus. Until then, misery will pursue us. Only resting in Mother are we safe.

The Essence Of Religion

(Report of a lecture delivered in America)

In France the "rights of man" was long a watchword of the race; in America the rights of women still beseech the public ear; in India we have concerned ourselves always with the rights of Gods.

The Vedanta includes all sects. We have a peculiar idea in India. Suppose I had a child; I should not teach him any religion, but the practice of concentrating his mind; and just one line of prayer — not prayer in your sense, but this: "I meditate on Him who is the Creator of the universe; may He enlighten my mind." Then, when old enough, he goes about hearing the different philosophies and teachings, till he finds that which seems the truth to him. He then becomes the Shishya or disciple of the Guru (teacher) who is teaching this truth. He may choose to worship Christ or Buddha or Mohammed: we recognise the rights of each of these, and the right of all souls to their own Ishta or chosen way. It is, therefore, quite possible for my son to be a Buddhist, my wife to be a Christian, and myself a Mohammedan at one and the same time with absolute freedom from friction.

We are all glad to remember that all roads lead to God; and that the reformation of the world does not depend upon all seeing God through our eyes. Our fundamental idea is that your doctrine cannot be mine, nor mine yours. I am my own sect. It is true that we have created a system of religion in India which we believe to be the only rational religious system extant; but our belief in its rationality rests upon its all-inclusion of the searchers after God; its absolute charity towards all forms of worship, and its eternal receptivity of those ideas trending towards the evolution of God in the universe. We admit the imperfection of our system, because the reality must be beyond all system; and in this admission lies the portent and promise of an eternal growth. Sects, ceremonies, and books, so far as they are the means of a man's realising his own nature, are all right; when he has realised that, he gives up everything. "I reject the Vedas!" is the last word of the Vedanta philosophy. Ritual, hymns, and scriptures, through which he has travelled to freedom, vanish for him. "So'ham, So'ham" — I am He, I am He — bursts from his lips, and to say "Thou" to God is blasphemy, for he is "one with the Father".

Personally, I take as much of the Vedas as agree with reason. Parts of the Vedas are apparently contradictory. They are not considered as inspired in the Western sense of the word, but as the sum total of the knowledge of God, omniscience, which we possess. But to say that only those books which we call the Vedas contain this knowledge is mere sophistry. We know it is shared in varying degrees by the scriptures of all sects. Manu says, that part only of the Vedas which agrees with reason is Vedas; and many of our philosophers have taken this view. Of all the scriptures of the world, it is the Vedas alone which declare that the study of the Vedas is secondary.

The real study is that "by which we realise the Unchangeable", and that is neither by reading, nor believing, nor reasoning, but by superconscious perception and Samâdhi. When a man has reached that perfect state, he is of the same nature as the Personal God: "I and my Father are one." He knows himself one with Brahman, the Absolute, and projects himself as does the Personal God. The Personal God is the Absolute looked at through the haze of Mâyâ — ignorance.

When we approach Him with the five senses, we can only see Him as the Personal God. The idea is that the Self cannot be objectified. How can the knower know himself? But he can cast a shadow, as it were, and the highest form of that shadow, that attempt of objectifying one's Self is the Personal God. The Self is the eternal subject, and we are eternally struggling to objectify that Self, and out of that struggle has come this phenomenon of the universe: that which we call matter. But these are weak attempts, and the highest objectification of the Self, possible to us, is the Personal God.

"An honest God's the noblest work of man", said one of your Western thinkers. God is as man is. No man can see God but through these human manifestations. Talk as you may, try as you may, you cannot think of God but as a man; and as you are, He is. An ignorant man was asked to make an image of the God Shiva; and after many days of hard struggle he succeeded only in manufacturing the image of a monkey! So, when we try to think of God as He is in His absolute perfection, we meet with miserable failure, because we are limited and bound by our present constitution to see God as man. If the buffaloes desire to worship God, they, in keeping with their own nature, will see Him as a huge buffalo; if a fish wishes to worship God, its concept of Him would inevitably be a big fish; and man must think of Him as man. Suppose man, the buffalo, and the fish represent so many different vessels; that these vessels all go to the sea of God to be filled, each according to its shape and capacity. In man the water takes the shape of man; in the buffalo the shape of the buffalo; and in the fish the shape of the fish; but in each of these vessels is the same water of the sea of God.

Two kinds of mind do not worship God as man — the human brute who has no religion, and the Paramahamsa who has transcended the limits of his own human nature. To him all nature has become his own Self; he alone can worship God as He is. The human brute does not worship because of his ignorance, and the Jivanmuktas (free souls) do not worship because they have realised God in themselves. "So'ham, So'ham" — I am He, I am He — they say; and how shall they worship themselves?

I will tell you a little story. There was once a baby lion left by its dying mother among some sheep. The sheep fed it and gave it shelter. The lion grew apace and said "Ba-a-a" when the sheep said "Ba-a-a". One day another lion came by. "What do you do here?" said the second lion in astonishment: for he heard the sheep-lion bleating with the rest. "Ba-a-a," said the other. "I am a little sheep, I am a little sheep, I am frightened." "Nonsense!" roared the first lion, "come with me; I will show you." And he took him to the side of a smooth stream and showed him that which was reflected therein. "You are a lion; look at me, look at the sheep, look at yourself." And the sheep-lion looked, and then he said, "Ba-a-a, I do not look like the sheep — it is true, I am a lion!" and with that he roared a roar that shook the hills to their depths.

That is it. We are lions in sheep's clothing of habit, we are hypnotised into weakness by our surroundings. And the province of Vedanta is the self-dehypnotisation. The goal to be reached is freedom. I disagree with the idea that freedom is obedience to the laws of nature. I do not understand what that means. According to the history of human progress, it is disobedience to nature that has constituted that progress. It may be said that the conquest of lower laws was through the higher, but even there the conquering mind was still seeking freedom; as soon as it found the struggle was through law, it wished to conquer that also. So the ideal is always freedom. The trees never disobey law. I never saw a cow steal. An oyster never told a lie. Yet these are not greater than man.

Obedience to law, in the last issue, would make of us simply matter — either in society, or in politics, or religion. This life is a tremendous assertion of freedom; excess of laws means death. No nation possesses so many laws as the Hindus, and the result is the national death. But the Hindus had one peculiar idea — they never made any doctrines or dogmas in religion; and the latter has had the greatest growth. Therein are we practical — wherein you are impractical — in our religion.

A few men come together in America and say, "We will have a stock company"; in five minutes it is done. In India twenty men may discuss a stock company for as many weeks, and it may not be formed; but if one believes that by holding up his hands in air for forty years he will attain wisdom, it will be done! So we are practical in ours, you in your way.

But the way of all ways to realisation is love. When one loves the Lord, the whole universe becomes dear to one, because it is all His. "Everything is His, and He is my Lover; I love Him", says the Bhakta. In this way everything becomes sacred to the Bhakta, because all things are His. How, then, may we hurt any one? How, then, may we not love another? With the love of God will come, as its effect, the love of every one in the long run. The nearer we approach God, the more do we begin to see that all things abide in Him, our heart will become a perennial fountain of love. Man is transformed in the presence of this Light of Love and realises at last the beautiful and inspiring truth that Love, Lover, and the Beloved are really one.

Sayings And Utterances

1. "Did Buddha teach that the many was real and the ego unreal, while orthodox Hinduism regards the One as the real, and the many as unreal?" the Swami was asked. "Yes", answered the Swami. "And what Ramakrishna Paramahamsa and I have added to this is, that the Many and the One are the same Reality, perceived by the same mind at different times and in different attitudes."

2. "Remember!" he said once to a disciple, "Remember! the message of India is always '*Not the soul for nature, but nature for the soul!*'"

3. "What the world wants today is twenty men and women who can dare to stand in the street yonder, and say that they possess nothing but God. Who will go? Why should one fear? If this is true, what else could matter? *If it is not true, what do our lives matter!*"

4. "Oh, how calm would be the work of one who really understood the divinity of man! For such, there is nothing to do, save to open men's eyes. All the rest does itself."

5. "He (Shri Ramakrishna) was contented simply to live that great life and to leave it to others to find the explanation!"

6. "Plans! Plans!" Swami Vivekananda explained in indignation, when one of his disciples had offered him some piece of worldly wisdom. "That is why . . . Western people can never create a religion! If any of you ever did, it was only a few Catholic saints who had no plans. Religion was never preached by planners!"

7. "Social life in the West is like a peal of laughter; but underneath, it is a wail. It ends in a sob. The fun and frivolity are all on the surface: really it is full of tragic intensity. Now here, it is sad and gloomy on the outside, but underneath are carelessness and merriment.

"We have a theory that the universe is God's manifestation of Himself just for fun, that the Incarnations came and lived here 'just for fun'. Play, it was all play. Why was Christ crucified? It was mere play. And so of life. Just play with the Lord. Say, "It is all play, it is all play". Do *you* do anything?"

8. "I am persuaded that a leader is not made in one life. He has to be born for it. For the difficulty is not in organisation and making plans; the test, the real test, of the leader, lies in holding widely different people together along the line of their common sympathies. And this can only be done unconsciously, never by trying."

9. In explanation of Plato's doctrine of Ideas, Swamiji said, "And so you see, all this is but a feeble manifestation of the great ideas, which alone, are real and perfect. Somewhere is an ideal for you, and here is an attempt to manifest it! The attempt falls short still in many ways. Still, go on! You will interpret the ideal some day."

10. Answering the remark of a disciple who felt that it would be better for her to come back to this life again and again and help the causes that were of interest to her instead of striving for personal salvation with a deep longing to get out of life, the Swami retorted quickly: "That's because you cannot overcome the idea of progress. But things do not grow better. They remain as they are; and we grow better by the changes we make in them."

11. It was in Almora that a certain elderly man, with a face full of amiable weakness, came and put him a question about Karma. What were they to do, he asked, whose Karma it was to see the strong oppress the weak? The Swami turned on him in surprised indignation. "Why, thrash the strong, of course!" he said, "You forget your own part in this Karma: Yours is always the right to rebel!"

12. "Ought one to seek an opportunity of death in defense of right, or ought one to take the lesson of the Gitâ and learn never to react?" the Swami was asked. "I am for no reaction", said the Swami, speaking slowly and with a long pause. Then he added " — for Sannyâsins. Self-defense for the householder!"

13. "It is a mistake to hold that with all men pleasure is the motive. Quite as many are born to seek after pain. Let us worship the Terror for Its own sake."

14. "Ramakrishna Paramahamsa was the only man who ever had the courage to say that we must speak to all men in their own language!"

15. "How I used to hate Kâli!" he said, referring to his own days of doubts in accepting the Kali ideal, "And all Her ways! That was the ground of my six years' fight — that I would not accept Her. But I had to accept Her at last! Ramakrishna Paramahamsa dedicated me to Her, and now I believe that She guides me in everything I do, and does with me what She will. . . . Yet I fought so long! I loved him, you see, and that was what held me. I saw his marvellous purity. . . . I felt his wonderful love. . . . His greatness had not

dawned on me then. All that came afterwards when I had given in. At that time I thought him a brain-sick baby, always seeing visions and the rest. I hated it. And then I, too, had to accept Her!

"No, the thing that made me do it is a secret that will die with me. I had great misfortunes at the time. . . . It was an opportunity. . . . She made a slave of me. Those were the very words: 'a slave of you'. And Ramakrishna Paramahamsa made me over to Her. . . . Strange! He lived only two years after doing that, and most of the time he was suffering. Not more than six months did he keep his own health and brightness.

"Guru Nanak was like that, you know, looking for the one disciple to whom he would give his power. And he passed over all his own family — his children were as nothing to him — till he came upon the boy to whom he gave it; and then he could die.

"The future, you say, will call Ramakrishna Paramahamsa an Incarnation of Kali? Yes, I think there's no doubt that She worked up the body of Ramakrishna for Her own ends.

"*You see, I cannot but believe that there is somewhere a great Power that thinks of Herself as feminine, and called Kali and Mother*. . . . And I believe in Brahman too. . . . But is it not always like that? Is it not the multitude of cells in the body that make up the personality, the many brain-centres, not the one, that produce consciousness? . . . Unity in complexity! Just so! And why should it be different with Brahman? It is Brahman. It is the One. And yet — and yet — it is the gods too!"

16. "The older I grow, the more everything seems to me to lie in manliness. This is my new gospel."

17. Referring to some European reference to cannibalism, as if it were a normal part of life in some societies, the Swami remarked, "That is not true! No nation ever ate human flesh, save as a religious sacrifice, or in war, out of revenge. Don't you see? That's not the way of gregarious animals! It would cut at the root of social life!"

18. "Sex-love and creation! These are at the root of most religions. And these in India are called Vaishnavism, and in the West Christianity. How few have dared to worship Death or Kali! Let us worship Death! Let us embrace the Terrible, because it is terrible, not asking that it be toned down. Let us take misery for misery's own sake!"

19. "The three cycles of Buddhism were five hundred years of the Law, five hundred years of images, and five hundred years of Tantras. You must not imagine that there was ever a religion in India called Buddhism with temples and priests of its own order! Nothing of the sort. It was always

within Hinduism. Only at one time the influence of Buddha was paramount, and this made the nation monastic."

20. "The conservative's whole ideal is *submission*. Your ideal is struggle. Consequently it is *we* who enjoy the life, and never you! You are always striving to change yours to something better; and before a millionth part of the change is carried out, you die. The Western ideal is to be doing; the Eastern to be suffering. The perfect life would be a wonderful harmony doing and suffering. But that can never be.

"In our system it is accepted that a man cannot have all he desires. Life is subjected to many restraints. This is ugly, yet it brings out points of light and strength. Our liberals see only the ugliness and try to throw it off. But they substitute something quite as bad; and the new custom takes as long as the old for us to work to its centres of strength.

"Will is not strengthened by change. It is weakened and enslaved by it. But we must be always absorbing. Will grows stronger by absorption. And consciously or unconsciously, will is the one thing in the world that we admire. Suttee is great in the eyes of the whole world, because of the will that it manifests.

"It is selfishness that we must seek to eliminate. I find that whenever I have made a mistake in my life, it has always been because *self* entered into the calculation. Where self has not been involved, my judgment has gone straight to the mark.

"Without self, there would have been no religious system. If man had not wanted anything for himself, do you think he would have had all this praying and worship? Why! he would never have thought of God at all, except perhaps for a little praise now and then, at the sight of a beautiful landscape or something. And that is the only attitude there ought to be. All praise and thanks. If only we were rid of self!

"You are quite wrong when you think that fighting is a sign of growth. It is not so at all. Absorption is the sign. Hinduism is a very genius of absorption. We have never cared for fighting. Of course we could strike a blow now and then, in defense of our homes! That was right. But we never cared for fighting for its own sake. Every one had to learn that. So let these races of newcomers whirl on! They'll all be taken into Hinduism in the end!"

21. "The totality of all souls, not the human alone, is the Personal God. The will of the Totality nothing can resist. It is what we know as law. And this is what we mean by Shiva and Kali and so on."

22. "Worship the Terrible! Worship Death! All else is vain. All struggle is vain. That is the last lesson. Yet this is not the coward's love of death, not

the love of the weak or the suicide. It is the welcome of the strong man who has sounded everything to its depths and knows that there is no alternative."

23. "I disagree with all those who are giving their superstitions back to my people. Like the Egyptologist's interest in Egypt, it is easy to feel an interest in India that is purely selfish. One may desire to see again the India of one's books, one's studies, one's dreams. My hope is to see again the strong points of that India, reinforced by the strong points of this age, only in a natural way. The new stage of things must be a growth from within.

"So I preach only the Upanishads. If you look, you will find that I have never quoted anything but the Upanishads. And of the Upanishads, it is only that One idea, strength. The quintessence of the Vedas and Vedanta and all lies in that one word. Buddha's teaching was non-resistance, or non-injury. But I think this is a better way of teaching the same thing. For behind that non-injury lay a dreadful weakness. It is weakness that conceives the idea of resistance. I do not think of punishing or escaping from a drop of sea-spray. It is nothing to me. Yet to the mosquito it would be serious. Now I would make all injury like that. Strength and fearlessness. My own ideal is that saint whom they killed in the Mutiny and who broke his silence, when stabbed to the heart, to say, 'And thou also art He!'

"But you may ask, 'What is the place of Ramakrishna in this scheme?'

"He is the method, that wonderful unconscious method! He did not understand himself. He knew nothing of England or the English, save that they were queer folk from over the sea. But he lived that great life: and I read the meaning. Never a word of condemnation for any! Once I had been attacking one of our sects of diabolists. I had been raving on for three hours, and he had listened quietly. 'Well, well!' said the old man as I finished, 'perhaps every house may have a backdoor. Who knows?'

"Hitherto the great fault of our Indian religion has lain in its knowing only two words: renunciation and Mukti. Only Mukti here! Nothing for the householder!

"But these are the very people whom I want to help. For are not all souls of the same quality? Is not the goal of all the same?

"And so strength must come to the nation through education."

24. The Puranas, the Swami considered, to be the effort of Hinduism to bring lofty ideas to the door of the masses. There had been only one mind in India that had foreseen this need, that of Krishna, probably the greatest man who ever lived.

The Swami said, "Thus is created a religion that ends in the worship of Vishnu, as the preservation and enjoyment of life, leading to the realisation of God. Our last movement, Chaitanyaism, you remember, was for enjoyment. At the same time Jainism represents the other extreme, the slow destruction of the body by self-torture. Hence Buddhism, you see, is reformed Jainism; and this is the real meaning of Buddha's leaving the company of the five ascetics. In India, in every age, there is a cycle of sects which represents every gradation of physical practice, from the extreme of self-torture to the extreme of excess. And during the same period will always be developed a metaphysical cycle, which represents the realisation of God as taking place by every gradation of means, from that of using the senses as an instrument to that of the annihilation of the senses. Thus Hinduism always consists, as it were, of two counter-spirals, completing each other, round a single axis.

"'Yes!' Vaishnavism says, 'it is all right — this tremendous love for father, for mother, for brother, husband, or child! It is all right, if only you will think that Krishna is the child, and when you give him food, that you are feeding Krishna!' This was the cry of Chaitanya, 'Worship God *through* the senses', as against the Vedantic cry, 'Control the senses! suppress the senses!'

"I see that India is a young and living organism. Europe is young and living. Neither has arrived at such a stage of development that we can safely criticise its institutions. They are two great experiments, neither of which is yet complete. In India we have social communism, with the light of Advaita — that is, spiritual individualism — playing on and around it; in Europe you are socially individualists, but your thought is dualistic, which is spiritual communism. Thus the one consists of socialist institutions hedged in by individualist thought, while the other is made up of individualist institutions within the hedge of communistic thought.

"Now we must help the Indian experiment as it is. Movements which do not attempt to help things as they are, are, from that point of view, no good. In Europe, for instance, I respect marriage as highly as non-marriage. Never forget that a man is made great and perfect as much by his faults as by his virtues. So we must not seek to rob a nation of its character, even if it could be proved that the character was all faults."

25. "You may always say that the image is God. The error you have to avoid is to think God is the image."

26. The Swami was appealed to on one occasion to condemn the fetishism of the Hottentot. "I do not know", he answered, "what fetishism is!" Then a lurid picture was hastily put before him of the object alternately worshipped, beaten, and thanked. "I do that!" he exclaimed. "Don't you

see," he went on, a moment later, in hot resentment of injustice done to the lowly and absent, "don't you see that there is no fetishism? Oh, your hearts are steeled, that you cannot see that the child is right! The child sees person everywhere. Knowledge robs us of the child's vision. But at last, through higher knowledge, we win back to it. He connects a living power with rocks, sticks, trees and the rest. And is there not a living Power behind them? It is *symbolism*, not fetishism! Can you not see?"

27. One day he told the story of Satyabhâmâ's sacrifice and how the word "Krishna", written on a piece of paper and thrown into the balance, made Krishna himself, on the other side, kick the beam. "Orthodox Hinduism", he began, "makes Shruti, the sound, everything. The *thing* is but a feeble manifestation of the pre-existing and eternal idea. So the *name* of God is everything: God Himself is merely the objectification of that idea in the eternal mind. Your own name is infinitely more perfect than the person you! The name of God is greater than God. Guard your speech!"

28. "I would not worship even the Greek Gods, for they were separate from humanity! Only those should be worshipped who are like ourselves but greater. The difference between the gods and me must be a difference only of degree."

29. "A stone falls and crushes a worm. Hence we infer that all stones, falling, crush worms. Why do we thus immediately reapply a perception? Experience, says one. But it happens, let us suppose, for the first time. Throw a baby into the air, and it cries. Experience from past lives? But why applied to the future? Because there is a real connection between certain things, a *pervasiveness*, only it lies with us to see that the quality neither overlaps, nor falls short of, the instance. On this discrimination depends all human knowledge.

"With regard to fallacies, it must be remembered that direct perception itself can only be a proof, provided the instrument, the method, and the persistence of the perception are all maintained pure. Disease or emotion will have the effect of disturbing the observation. *Therefore direct perception itself is but a mode of inference*. Therefore all human knowledge is uncertain and may be erroneous. Who is a true witness? He is a true witness to whom the thing said is a direct perception. Therefore the Vedas are true, because they consist of the evidence of competent persons. But is this power of perception peculiar to any? No! The Rishi, the Aryan, and the Mlechchha all alike have it.

"Modern Bengal holds that evidence is only a special case of direct perception, and that analogy and parity of reasoning are only bad inferences. Therefore, of actual proofs there are only two, direct perception and inference.

"One set of persons, you see, gives priority to the external manifestation, the other to the internal idea. Which is prior, the bird to the egg, or the egg to the bird? Does the oil hold the cup or the cup the oil? This is a problem of which there is no solution. Give it up! Escape from Maya!"

30. "Why should I care if the world itself were to disappear? According to my philosophy, that, you know, would be a very good thing! But, in fact, all that is against me must be with me in the end. Am I not Her soldier?"

31. "Yes, my own life is guided by the enthusiasm of a certain great personality, but what of that? Inspiration was never filtered out to the world through one man!

"It is true I believe Ramakrishna Paramahamsa to have been inspired. But then I am myself inspired also. And you are inspired. And your disciples will be; and theirs after them; and so on, to the end of time!

"Don't you see that the age for esoteric interpretation is over? For good or for ill, that day is vanished, never to return. Truth, in the future, is to be open to the world!"

32. "Buddha made the fatal mistake of thinking that the whole world could be lifted to the height of the Upanishads. And self-interest spoilt all. Krishna was wiser, because He was more politic. But Buddha would have no compromise. The world before now has seen even the Avatâra ruined by compromise, tortured to death for want of recognition, and lost. But Buddha would have been worshipped as God in his own lifetime, all over Asia, for a moment's compromise. And his reply was only: 'Buddhahood is an achievement, not a person!' Verily was He the only man is the world who was ever quite sane, the only sane man ever born!"

33. People had told the Swami in the West that the greatness of Buddha would have been more appealing, had he been crucified! This he stigmatised as "Roman brutality", and pointed out, "The lowest and most animal liking is for action. Therefore the world will always love the epic. Fortunately for India, however, she has never produced a Milton, with his 'hurled headlong down the steep abyss'! The whole of that were well exchanged for a couple of lines of Browning!" It had been this epic vigour of the story, in his opinion, that had appealed to the Roman. The crucifixion it was that carried Christianity over the Roman world. "Yes, Yes!" he reiterated. "You Western folk want *action*! You cannot yet perceive the poetry of every common little incident in life! What beauty could be greater than that of the story of the young mother coming to Buddha with her dead boy? Or the incident of the

goats? You see the Great Renunciation was not new in India! . . . But *after Nirvâna*, look at the poetry!

"It is a wet night, and he comes to the cowherd's hut and gathers in to the wall under the dripping eaves. The rain is pouring down and the wind rising.

"Within, the cowherd catches a glimpse of a face through the window and thinks, 'Ha, ha! Yellow garb! stay there! It's good enough for you!' And then he begins to sing.

"'My cattle are housed, and the fire burns bright. My wife is safe, and my babes sleep sweet! Therefore ye may rain, if ye will, O clouds, tonight!'

"And the Buddha answers from without, "My mind is controlled: my senses are all gathered in; my heart firm. Therefore ye may rain, if ye will, O clouds, tonight!'

"Again the cowherd: 'The fields are reaped, and the hay is fast in the barn. The stream is full, and the roads are firm. Therefore ye may rain, if ye will, O clouds, tonight.'

"And so it goes on, till at last the cowherd rises, in contrition and wonder, and becomes a disciple.

"Or what would be more beautiful than the barber's story?

The Blessed One passed by my house,
my house — the Barber's!
I ran, but He turned and awaited me,
Awaited *me* — the Barber!
"I said, 'May I speak, O Lord, with Thee?'
And He said 'Yes!'
'Yes!' to *me* — the Barber!
"And I said, 'Is Nirvana for such as I?'
And He said 'Yes!'
Even for *me* — the Barber!
"And I said, 'May I follow after Thee?'
And He said, 'Oh yes!'
Even *I* — the Barber!
And I said, 'May I stay, O Lord, near Thee?'
"And He said, 'Thou mayest!'
Even to *me* — the poor Barber!"

34. "The great point of contrast between Buddhism and Hinduism lies in the fact that Buddhism said, 'Realise all this as illusion', while Hinduism said, 'Realise that within the illusion is the Real.' Of *how* this was to be done, Hinduism never presumed to enunciate any rigid law. The Buddhist command could only be carried out through monasticism; the Hindu might be fulfilled through any state of life. All alike were roads to the One Real. One of the highest and greatest expressions of the Faith is put into the mouth of a butcher, preaching by the orders of a married woman to a Sannyasin. Thus Buddhism became the religion of a monastic order, but Hinduism, in spite of its exaltation of monasticism, remains ever the religion of faithfulness to duty, whatever it be, as the path by which man may attain God."

35. "Lay down the rules for your group and formulate your ideas," the Swami said, dealing with the monastic ideal for women, "and put in a little universalism, if there is room for it. But remember that not more than half a dozen people in the whole world are ever at any time ready for this! There must be room for sects, as well as for rising above sects. You will have to manufacture your own tools. Frame laws, but frame them in such a fashion that when people are ready to do without them, they can burst them asunder. Our originality lies in combining perfect freedom with perfect authority. This can be done even in monasticism."

36. "Two different races mix and fuse, and out of them rises one strong distinct type. This tries to save itself from admixture, and here you see the beginning of caste. Look at the apple. The best specimens have been produced by crossing; but once crossed, we try to preserve the variety intact."

37. Referring to education of girls in India he said, "In worship of the gods, you must of course use images. But you can change these. Kali need not always be in one position. Encourage your girls to think of new ways of picturing Her. Have a hundred different conceptions of Saraswati. Let them draw and model and paint their own ideas.

"In the chapel, the pitcher on the lowest step of the altar must be always full of water, and lights in great Tamil butter-lamps must be always burning. If, in addition, the maintenance of perpetual adoration could be organised, nothing could be more in accord with Hindu feeling.

"But the ceremonies employed must themselves be Vedic. There must be a Vedic altar, on which at the hour of worship to light the Vedic fire. And the children must be present to share in the service of oblation. This is a rite which would claim the respect of the whole of India.

"Gather all sorts of animals about you. The cow makes a fine beginning. But you will also have dogs and cats and birds and others. Let the children have a time for going to feed and look after these.

"Then there is the sacrifice of learning. That is the most beautiful of all. Do you know that every book is holy in India, not the Vedas alone, but the English and Mohammedan also? All are sacred.

"Revive the old arts. Teach your girls fruit-modelling with hardened milk. Give them artistic cooking and sewing. Let them learn painting, photography, the cutting of designs in paper, and gold and silver filigree and embroidery. See that everyone knows something by which she can earn a living in case of need.

"And never forget Humanity! The idea of a humanitarian man-worship exists in nucleus in India, but it has never been sufficiently specialised. Let your students develop it. Make poetry, make art, of it. Yes, a daily worship at the feet of beggars, after bathing and before the meal, would be a wonderful practical training of heart and hand together. On some days, again, the worship might be of children, of your own pupils. Or you might borrow babies and nurse and feed them. What was it that Mâtâji (Tapaswini Mataji, foundress of the Mahâkâli Pâthasâlâ, Calcutta.) said to me? 'Swamiji! I have no help. But these blessed ones I worship, and they will take me to salvation!' She feels, you see, that she is serving Umâ in the Kumâri, and that is a wonderful thought, with which to begin a school."

38. "Love is always a manifestation of bliss. The least shadow of pain falling upon it is always a sign of physicality and selfishness."

39. "The West regards marriage as consisting in all that lies beyond the legal tie, while in India it is thought of as a bond thrown by society round two people to unite them together for all eternity. Those two must wed each other, whether they will or not, in life after life. Each acquires half of the merit of the other. And if one seems in this life to have fallen hopelessly behind, it is for the other only to wait and beat time, till he or she catches up again!"

40. "Consciousness is a mere film between two oceans, the subconscious and the superconscious."

41. "I could not believe my own ears when I heard Western people talking so much of consciousness! Consciousness? What does consciousness matter! Why, it is nothing compared with the unfathomable depths of the subconscious and the heights of the superconscious! In this I could never be misled, for had I not seen Ramakrishna Paramahamsa gather in ten minutes,

from a man's subconscious mind, the whole of his past, and determine from that his future and his powers?"

42. "All these (visions etc.) are side issues. They are not true Yoga. They may have a certain usefulness in establishing indirectly the truth of our statements. Even a little glimpse gives faith that there is something behind gross matter. Yet those who spend time on such things run into grave dangers.

"These (psychic developments) are *frontier questions*! There can never be any certainty or stability of knowledge reached by their means. Did I not say they were 'frontier questions'? The boundary line is always shifting!"

43. "Now on the Advaitic side it is held that the soul neither comes nor goes, and that all these spheres or layers of the universe are only so many varying products of Âkâsha and Prâna. That is to say, the lowest or most condensed is the Solar Sphere, consisting of the visible universe, in which Prana appears as physical force, and Akasha as sensible matter. The next is called the Lunar Sphere, which surrounds the Solar Sphere. This is not the moon at all, but the habitation of the gods; that is to say, Prana appears in it as psychic forces, and Akasha as Tanmatras or fine particles. Beyond this is the Electric Sphere; that is to say, a condition inseparable from Akasha, and you can hardly tell whether electricity is force or matter. Next is the Brahmaloka, where there is neither Prana nor Akasha, but both are merged into the mind-stuff, the primal energy. And here — there being neither Prana nor Akasha — the Jiva contemplates the whole universe as Samashti or the sum total of Mahat or mind. This appears as Purusha, an abstract Universal Soul, yet not the Absolute, for still there is multiplicity. From this the Jiva finds at last that Unity which is the end. Advaitism says that these are the visions which arise in succession before the Jiva, who himself neither goes nor comes, and that in the same way this present vision has been projected. The projection (Srishti) and dissolution must take place in the same order, only one means going backward and the other coming out.

"Now, as each individual can only see his own universe, that universe is created with his bondage and goes away with his liberation, although it remains for others who are in bondage. Now, name and form constitute the universe. A wave in the ocean is a wave only in so far as it is bound by name and form. If the wave subsides, it is the ocean, but that name-and-form has immediately vanished forever, so that the name and form of a wave could never be without the water that was fashioned into the wave by them. Yet the name and form themselves were not the wave; they die as soon as ever it returns to water, but other names and forms live on in relation to other waves. This name-and-form is called Maya and the water is Brahman. The wave was nothing but water all the time, yet as a wave it had the name and form. Again this name-and-form cannot remain for one moment separated from the wave, although the wave, as water, can remain eternally separate from name and form. But because the name and form can never be separated, they can never be said to exist. Yet they are not zero. This is called Maya."

44. "I am the servant of the servants of the servants of Buddha. Who was there ever like him? — the Lord — who never performed one action for himself — with a heart that embraced the whole world! So full of pity that he — prince and monk — would give his life to save a little goat! So loving that he sacrificed himself to the hunger of a tigress! — to the hospitality of a pariah and blessed him! And he came into my room when I was a boy, and I fell at his feet! For I knew it was the Lord Himself!"

45. "He (Shuka) is the ideal Paramahamsa. To him alone amongst men was it given to drink a handful of the waters of that one undivided Ocean of Sat-Chit-Ânanda — Existence, Knowledge, and Bliss Absolute! Most saints die, having heard only the thunder of its waves upon the shore. A few gain the vision, and still fewer, taste of It. But he drank of the Sea of Bliss!"
46. "What is this idea of Bhakti without renunciation? It is most pernicious."

47. "We worship neither pain nor pleasure. We seek through either to come at that which transcends them both."

48. "Shankaracharya had caught the rhythm of the Vedas, the national cadence. Indeed I always imagine that he had some vision such as mine when he was young, and recovered the ancient music that way. Anyway, his whole life's work is nothing but that, the throbbing of the beauty of the Vedas and the Upanishads."

49. "Though the love of a mother is in some ways greater, yet the whole world takes the love of man and woman as the type (of the soul's relation to God). *No other has such tremendous idealising power*. The beloved actually becomes what he is imagined to be. This love transforms its object."

50. "Is it so easy to be Janaka — to sit on a throne absolutely unattached, caring nothing for wealth or fame, for wife or child? One after another in the West has told me that he has reached this. But I could only say, 'Such great men are not born in India!'".

51. "Never forget to say to yourself and to teach to your children, as the difference between a firefly and the blazing sun, between the infinite ocean and a little pond, between a mustard seed and the mountain Meru, such is the difference between the householder and the Sannyasin!

"Everything is fraught with fear: Renunciation alone is fearless.

"Blessed be even the fraudulent Sâdhus and those who have failed to carry out their vows, inasmuch as they also have witnessed to their ideal and so are in some degree the cause of the success of others!

"Let us never, never, forget our ideal!"

52. "The river is pure that flows, the monk is pure that goes!"

53. "The Sannyasin who thinks of gold, to desire it, commits suicide."

54. "What do I care if Mohammed *was* a good man, or Buddha? Does that altar my goodness or evil? Let us be good for our own sake on our own responsibility."

55. "You people in this country are so afraid of losing your in-di-vid-u-al-i-ty! Why, you are not individuals yet. When you realise your whole nature, you will attain your true individuality, not before. There is another thing I am constantly hearing in this country, and that is that we should live in harmony with nature. Don't you know that all the progress ever made in the world was made by conquering nature? We are to resist nature at every point if we are to make any progress."

56. "In India they tell me I ought not to teach Advaita Vedanta to the people at large; but I say, I can make even a child understand it. You cannot begin too early to teach the highest spiritual truths."

57. "The less you read, the better. Read the Gita and other good works on Vedanta. That is all you need. The present system of education is all wrong. The mind is crammed with facts before it knows how to think. Control of the mind should be taught first. If I had my education to get over again and had any voice in the matter, I would learn to master my mind first, and then gather facts if I wanted them. It takes people a long time to learn things because they can't concentrate their minds at will."

58. "If a bad time comes, what of that? The pendulum must swing back to the other side. But that is no better. The thing to do is to stop it."